NIGHTBOAT BOOKS
NEW YORK

TEETER

KIMBERLY
ALIDIO

ISBN: 978-1-643-62173-9

Cover design and interior typesetting by Rissa Hochberger
Typeset in Neue Haas Grotesk

Cataloging-in-publication data is available from the Library of Congress

Nightboat Books
New York
www.nightboat.org

For

Presentación Viray Garcia Sison

Rosalinda Garcia Sison Alidio

Veniedo Alimario Alvero Alidio

& Armand Jay Alidio

The inner sound of the poet protects the poet.
        — BARBARA GUEST

This, whatever this is, is the future interrupting the past ... // Tonight a body also produces (produced) itself as sound
        — MÓNICA DE LA TORRE

The sounds that move at a time .... Mother, my first sound.
        — THERESA HAK KYUNG CHA

The sedative present, tugging, sucking, and many-voiced
        — JENNIFER MOXLEY

in questo interregno si verificano i fenomeni morbosi piú svariati
        — ANTONIO GRAMSCI

That is to say, the noise that it makes is part of the meaning.
        — KAMAU BRATHWAITE

There is almost not an interval.
        — GERTRUDE STEIN

Her matter inserted, a motive, is always somewhere else, exiting one language, another without intent, translated as heart.
        — MEI-MEI BERSSENBRUGGE

A reel played backwards, that's the future .... No object can compete with a sound's intimacy .... A few seconds of love create havoc in History.
        — ETEL ADNAN

HEARING

A setting of sun tones says

here's an end of one the start of another
off-key gets acoustic so a skip can process
the voice a catgut pulled high by creek tide
as caterwaul of light in successive waves
death echo out there in the prehistoric weeds
isn't recourse to one's person. An arc pauses
before its penumbra, alternating gills of exhaling fern

then pretty overtaken at 6:48 & broken into staggered
phonemic vocalizing. I saw another usage of the term *pneuma*
the other day, the first appearance since pneuma of
Hannah. Sustaining harmonic tone behind it all
fades to become less music. What's machine, what's
vocal track. A screeching repeated, a new underdrone
A raindrop vocal opens into breathing
the bass static contrasts with the highest
vocal pitch, girl, you're gonna hurt those cords
hurt that tract. At 37:00, a radar signal with melody
convulsive spitting. The pneuma is still
there. Embodied with a machine
choral excitement to glissando tone at 43:00 onward

       spittle
       airplane sounds
       blubber
release a lock of hair over the mic
in ecstatic dance the torso makes a steady
tone in a short circular distance relative to the mic
shifting pitch with proximity along an axis
she is the variant sharp upstroke positive
velocity the slow-wave sleep
we are the mic stationary in hand post equinoctial
north wintering into layers of looped vocalizing with
machine a helicopter a chopper syncopates at
our side a spectrum of scream & song peaks at
13:06 we are a rumble fed into differential
sound interrupting with silence singles out
a tone huffed out

rather than a cross-sound wrenching me out of noise
Even a soundless text requires multiple channels. The
percussion structure regularizes by 0:49 & is fully arrived
by 1:07. By 1:30, a new layer. Audience conversations form
undercurrents. Refrain gains variation & static density before
3:00. Here are maracas & synths. 4:07: a break allows density
its recognition. At 5:40 there's bass static. I'm still listening in a
spaced out way of suspended thought. 8:04: an anthemic chorus
from far away. The space is there to fathom traversing, or not
As if a sun has set, the camera angle obscures the artists
Bodies buzz circularly to navigate the skin blob's
numb spots, their muffled response from oiled exposure. Bass
comes back in at 16:34 & slows down. 19:05: a deep heartbeat
with a small woodblock percussion & a shaken percussive
thing then vocal calls. Limbed shadows get a bit uncertain
because layers are mostly dissonant. Cohering for a
moment & then not & overheard chatter begins again

an expansive internalization of projection in a room or
on a street, a texture of internal-external perceptual
activity, the sound of presence, the roots of language
before it is born on the tip of the tongue

a poem-dream of funny vital dimensions, vocalizing to
sprout more dimensions, hearing's text wants
further aural aspects

resonances when ear & grapheme & hum
come into & drift out of phase

auditory dimensions that would be noisy & spatial
are distilled. I like this static then hate it two minutes in

aware of vocalizing at about 2:50. Of noise admirably
continuous, allowing aloud adaptation by being sustained
by sustaining itself a ground for layers & variation

but sometimes the static is at a frequency right at
some edge of dislike. Gives way at 5:45

The vocal tract co-activates analog-
digital processing co-activates the
acoustic space co-activates ephemeral
diegetic sound

Takes us back to the borderline
moment when the word has not
yet been born. Sounding silently
activates the larynx minutely

A practice of silent reading. The not-
sounding not-uttering fails & fails until
the time before language begins relating
She mimicks the speaking

Minutely activating bypasses sudden &
familiar absence in the throat to huff with
the void as to sound is the sounds of
the world being uttered

running into the same problem of
tracking flows in listening. The book vs all
other delivery systems keeps flipping
hierarchies whereas a sound-engineered or
raw, unproduced performance
document crawls across platforms &
venues so I navigate lists on Bandcamp,
Spotify, YouTube & Ubuweb

A melody contour repeats

precisely into its own transformation
[inhale] aTHROUGH•beNEATH•thra
THROUGH•beNEATH•thraTHROUGH•be
NEATH•aTHROUGH•beNEATH•aTHROUGH•
beNEATH•thraTHROUGH•beNEATH•thra
THROUGHbeNEATH•aTHROUGH•beNEATH•
LIT At first, Sound variegated through
beneath lit stresses the first word then
sort of pushes together the last two
beneath lit is a portmanteau. A variation
splits apart the pushed-together
words seeming to rush syllables

aBOVE•beNEATH   aBUB•beNEATH•LIT

aBOVE•beNEATH•aBOVE•beNEATH•LIT•aBUB•be
NEATH•aBUB•beNEATH•aBUB•beNEATH•aBUB•
beNEATH•aBUB•beNEATH•aBUB•beNEATH•a
BUB•beNEATH•aBUB•beNEATH•aBUB•be
NEATH•LIT A writing, a recording of
vocal signals into sign, shorthand
waveform-deviations etched as deviations

A recording of recording

Choreo-phonography: of both
Greek & uncertain origin, both dance &
voice, a rejoicing of dancers & voices under
constraint, both improvised &
Black chant. Translation turns
literature into an ephemeral experience
situating it close to music or
dance – in time. The pitch intonation
beNEATH•LIT can't be scored the
way I transcribe my hearing. A vocal
rigor & recording pops. Can you hear it?

Lingual music of the seaside & so forth over a soft & uneven
pulsing clip until the squeaks & whats overlap. Occasional minor
electric guitar chords. I hate the snow! I just learned after all these
years my son hates the beach! The whats disappear & hey! hey! hey!
punctuates the flock of high pitched calls. This noisy discourse also
subsides. What're you gonna do in Georgia? people ask, as if
they're gonna visit. A suite of bongos & cymbals tells jokes
asks for hot dogs, says hi to Donny. The flock higher in the sky now
circling over the whats of sand crabs, herons, & plastic pails

High pitched sounds, bubbles & popping, smacking,

Vibration is here
Expressively performative voices in
some kind of animated dialogue. With the sssshhhhh of
ambience etc. The high-low, woah-woah, slow-fast
eh-ah-eh-ahehah, taktaktak mix of percussion
instrumentation, vocalizations, sound effects that
place communication in noisescape

What waits to be
acknowledged as
wood Waited
the world of
revelation Of
reception what
we do now is
Preparation of
the head &
heart to receive
A universe In

time a micro
phone set At Boston
Harbor to live
among live Sound
piped through
telephone Wire
hundreds of
miles in
one's Room in
Kingston NY
a tone of Not to
pick up boat
horns or water
Waves or birds
but to dream
Music that triggers
another in The

listener a third Ear
or other's tympani
Autotheory's daily
sense of another
Environment for three
years prepares a
dawning I begin To
live in this tone
Conscious of a
resonant Third
breathing out
from Cells
the steady Periodic
sound of another
City not a closed
universe but
a universe in Time

& its message: *on time*. One track of sampled phrases
the arcing pitch of the streetcar engine, the page-flipping
on a table, the bell resonance. One track for a looped beat
& rumbling undercurrent. A third for distortion counterpoint
Essay as drone festival on a moving train. The blur of brick
wall to green tree. The phone someone is shouting into, "I'm
in Rhinecliff!" Screeching slow down, the stop & the
speeding up, the motion is the sound & vice versa
Ongoingness marked by the no-longer. Some tracks with
teeth removed. A frenzy & a thickness help hear the gaps
a whoosh cuffs the ears. Of wind, labored breathing, dialogue
Footsteps keep time. The ear's repertoire, with varied fluencies
composes footsteps, streetcar bells, bird calls, cicadas &
engines as speech modulators. One audio capture of
an iPhone video recording of a walk through an alley &
another of an iPhone video recording on Bowen Trail
Isolated vocalizations, bird imitations cut with laughter
Then graphemes suspended in negative space

pass away & the summer stations. Of the indelible & the
tremulous, both a fellowship & an indictment. Slowing down to
idle, swaying in suspension, a momentum that can spiral to a
stop or start up. Forward for ten seconds & undo to get
somewhere. To mirror, to double evanescence. Of the
diptych, non-binary binary, the &/or, refusal to decide, multiple
in the dual, refusal of one & space of other. The swampy
bugginess of endless rain flips the scorch & wildfires of the
place just left. On earth anywhere stresses the body
Romance doesn't overwhelm ecosystem but only some know
a sensory letdown moving away from the ends of the
earth, where friend scarcity & giant ancient plants daily invite
the paranormal. Turbid, brackish, super confluent, my new river
homes me for others. Each sound a dislodged world
skirting close to a god complex, fade up into the ringing
without the percussive start. Feet when wheeled or jarred by a knee
Of the jolting screech pattern before the stationed hum

starting up, live delay. A continuous military aircraft. Starting north on
N. 1st, west on E. 2nd, south on Herbert, one of many glorious alleys
east on University. A walk is linear in one sense, circular when return
meets departure, still to time & place in memory. A recorded
soundwalk a few weeks into quarantine. The grief of both!
The vertigo of sonic memory suggests you've gone off the map
The passing of one with the name of a month. After the passing of one with
a professional pronoun different from the personal. To write in
word pairs one too many words. To teeter. Verbs & adjectives in
noisy twos. By whose hand does an author die? J, how have you
reconciled the theory of M's self-care when M is known for taking
her own life? Loop by cut-&-paste every ten seconds. Reverse every
duplicate. Living is an act of cession, letting it slip from grasp. To decide is
lonely. To find the third. Of a walk interrupted by looking. To train the
ear only to the time of each decay until the body gives out some
industry. Of stations & a train for embarking & disembarking

wandering at a measured pace, whispering that seems
from the audience but now part of the piece, more footsteps
semi-ASMR, room ambience, bird sound, the whispers are
metalingual, deictic, diegetic, the bird sounds mechanical
Sound of an engine starting up, an olden machine, then
a hand brushing across a page. The rip: a book arranges
ripped text. A performance opens with rips, vocalized
consonant-heavy phonemes. 1:46 begins the drone
An ambulance siren enters. Live voice so modulated
so formal, it's interchangeable with a recorded one
The same clipped plosives, the t's, throaty /ehhm/
aerated /huhhh/. About four minutes in, recorded voice
is layered in with the sustained organ-like chord
What is it called when a sound seems to circle, like
bees or tinkly beads. A salt shaker, shaken idiophone!
An airplane engine-like bass. Propellers. Precise
convincing vocalization. Drone returns. Vocal distortions
Feet crunching on snow. 29 minutes at Harvard in
2011: silence, then confesses, "That was it"

site, shapes a gesture engaging the site's frequencies
Circularity tracing the sound arch: hollow bodies of
cicada or a bridge site, swivel motions of interventionist
waves along the curvilinear bodies. Lateral motion
sustains perception. Perception can escape the sensorial
& neural organs that activate it & move along, against
Bounce, echo, refrain, mimic, record & play back its
sideways movements. Some of the above was written in
the recess, 24 minutes in. Some of the above is written in
the recess, 20 minutes in

Ongoing intonations of sympathetic complaint. Sardonic humor marks
the bind of naming a violation of some sort, probably work related, now named
microaggression. Afternoon shadows against a wall. Sun noise constantly moves
through the filters of tree branch & window blind. Of disassociating from subordinate
placement, which I say is *normal* to the person on the phone. Intimacy is having no
memory of who I was talking to

Where a person on the other end of a crisis survival phone call lacks

a voice & name hints of shared institutional affiliation. Into that break comes
another phone call, What you do & what you will continue to do will
exceed the structural violence of academia. The point of what
you do is absolutely bound up with the person who rigorously
& beautifully confounds the disciplinary foundations of the
imperial university & who is a key contributor to ending that
violence, transmitted to the edge of a former bed, by the angled narrow
beam of sun & suspended dust, above a noise floor

You can make a shape, cut then paste it into a file

isolate a certain formant or upper partial, turn speech into total tonalism. In a
moment of pure listening, I once spoke over simultaneous outbursts in chorus with
a cacophony of girls

Another video posted on my social media

account is a slow approach to an ancient live oak several years ago. The male cicada
wails out of the ground of periodic dog days. Layering the phone call with
intermittent whine maps a transitive noisescape from
an old living room out into the greenbelt. The complaint floor gives out a laugh's
short attack. Intermittent bitter release high out into the same-old

sound vibrates gas   sound vibrates solid   sound vibrates liquid   changes   a   medium's pressure   transmits   radiates   a number of waves   from one crest to another per second is frequency   music's frequency ratios form simple fractions   a   noise   frequency   is seen thru a probability distribution   a sound compares to a color   a sound abstracts into a waveform   a musical waveform makes a patterned gradation in volume a noise waveform makes jagged irregularity   music has mathematical infinity   out of which only a handful of overtones matter   noise lacks a dominant frequency we can see

sound vibrates gas
sound vibrates solid
sound vibrates liquid
changes a medium's pressure
transmits
radiates
a number of waves
from one crest to another
per second is frequency
music's frequency ratios form simple fractions
a noise frequency is seen thru a probability distribution
a sound compares to a color
a sound abstracts into a waveform
a musical waveform makes a patterned gradation in volume
a noise waveform makes jagged irregularity
music has mathematical infinity
out of which only a handful of overtones matter
noise lacks a dominant frequency we can see

music is sound of discrete structure
noise is sound of continuous structure
a noise particle is in constant motion
with perfectly elastic collisions
in random directions
& a distribution of speeds
a vibration is unpredictable beyond measure
a presence of noise
the mouth radiates into the air
its formant regions create sonorance
with articulators
like the epiglottis at the windpipe
pharynx or throat dangling the uvula
soft palate
hard palate
back of the gum-line
gum-line just behind the teeth
edge of the teeth upper lip
articulators resonate their shapes & positions
as air pressure drops to modify an internal airstream
rising from the diaphragm
oscillating vocal cords
across the larynx

21

music is sound of discrete structure　　　noise is sound of continuous structure　　　a noise
particle is in constant motion　with　perfectly elastic collisions　　in random directions　&　　　a
distribution of speeds　　　a vibration is unpredictable beyond measure　　　a presence of noise
the mouth radiates into the air　　　its formant regions create sonorance　with articulators　　　like
the epiglottis at the windpipe　pharynx or throat dangling the uvula　soft palate　　hard palate　back
of the gum-line　　　gum-line just behind the teeth　　　edge of the teeth upper lip　articulators
resonate their shapes & positions　　as air pressure drops　to modify an internal airstream
rising from the diaphragm　　oscillating vocal cords　　across the larynx　　　up　through
abdominals　chest muscles rib cage lungs windpipe trachea voice box　　airflow is smooth or laminar
airflow is steadily turbulent　above the threshold of airspeed　　below　the　threshold　is　nil　voicing
"fin"　"thin"　"sin"　"shin"　"hello!"　　voiceless consonants hold vocal chords open　　do
not activate the folds　breath voicing is a very gentle rustle　"hat"　whisper voicing is aperiodic waves
"ssshhhhhh"　on all sides from innumerable tongues　　a dismal universal hiss　　the sound of
public scorn

up through abdominals
chest muscles
rib cage
lungs
windpipe
trachea voice box
airflow is smooth or laminar
airflow is steadily turbulent
above the threshold of airspeed
below the threshold is nil voicing
"fin"　"thin"　"sin"　"shin"　"hello!"
voiceless consonants hold vocal chords open
do not activate the folds
breath voicing is a very gentle rustle
"hat"
whisper voicing is aperiodic waves
"ssshhhhhh"
on all sides from innumerable tongues
a dismal universal hiss
the sound of public scorn

Wendy tells me
if you're good, you can read
"I live in the state of California"
from a spectrogram
the simplest type of soundwave is a pure vowel
a single frequency
a single voiced sound
a pure sound is a shape exactly repeating
from cycle to cycle
it doesn't exist
maybe with a tuning fork
voiced consonants are a mix of periodic & aperiodic waves
oscillating vocal folds
phonemes in combination make their own graphed shape
consonants too have their feelings
a very new newborn's cry is more music than noise
although some cries are rough
as in "vehement"
the word "ambience" has both pure sound & turbulence
cries have less interruption
the high drama of primate calls forms a melodic gestalt
in a scale-trained brain

22

Wendy tells me   if you're good, you can read   "I live in the state of California" from a spectrogram
the simplest type of soundwave is a pure vowel   a single frequency   a single voiced sound a
pure sound is a shape exactly repeating   from cycle to cycle   it doesn't exist maybe with a tuning
fork   voiced consonants are a mix of periodic & aperiodic waves   oscillating vocal folds   phonemes
in combination make their own graphed shape   consonants too have their feelings   a very new
newborn's cry is more music than noise   although some cries are rough   as in "vehement"
the word "ambience" has both pure sound & turbulence   cries have less interruption   the high
drama of primate calls forms a melodic gestalt   in a scale-trained brain   signal analysis gives the
rest of us   empirical evidence of the musics of the libidinal chthonic   spike-flutter flutter-spike
spike-spike   flutter-flutter

signal analysis gives the rest of us
empirical evidence
of the musics of the libidinal chthonic
spike-flutter
flutter-spike
spike-spike
flutter-flutter

a dog also makes the air speak
late-term fetal laryngeal & respiratory systems grow
resonant with motherese
stirring airflow up in the diaphragm
through abdominals
chest muscles
rib cage
lungs
trachea windpipe
larynx voice box
oscillating vocal cords as pressure drops
& modified by resonating shapes & positions of upper lip
edge of the teeth
behind the teeth
gumline
back of the gumline
hard palate
soft palate
uvula at the throat or pharynx
epiglottis at the trachea windpipe
radiating out the mouth

a short inspiratory noise's shape-melody
transposes across tones
expands or compresses in time
a single fundamental frequency contour
gains multiples in segments imitates motherese
as cries cooing babbling
newborns prefer motherese
& native tongue
they can discern semitones
beat cycles pitch rise & pitch fall
through soft & hardware
discrete parts & continuous parts

a dog also makes the air speak   late-term fetal laryngeal & respiratory systems grow   resonant with motherese   stirring airflow up in the diaphragm   through abdominals chest muscles rib cage lungs trachea windpipe larynx voice box   oscillating vocal cords as pressure drops   & modified by resonating shapes & positions of upper lip   edge of the teeth   behind the teeth gumline   back of the gumline   hard palate soft palate uvula at the throat or pharynx epiglottis at the trachea windpipe   radiating out the mouth

orderliness & jaggedness
stomps percussively
to dampened drone
in customary chant
at the common fire
speaking is pregnant with echo
soundwaves vibrating air also vibrate
solids liquids gasses from whence they came
glottal pauses between arcs resemble
psychoacoustic boundaries of phonemes
plosives
conclusives
stops
a prosody
starts to block
the vocal track from air
interrupt a vowel wail
to speak

sentences start & end a vowel can have a pattern forever
infinitude & chokehold
in the channel for emotive conative phatic & poetic func-
tions
we track in lament
an infant's late-term fetal hearing
our hearing searches out their hearing
in my poem
an abstraction of my voice
you may search out
my childhood hearing
dream
I was a baby who spoke seven
languages but none of them my parents used
sorry to wake you
in my dream department box
Mauricio left me three dozen dream eggs
& five individually wrapped Cadbury dream eggs
my dream name
according to my dream chair
over the dream loudspeaker
is Amber Alidio
can we hear from her now
noise calls up the very question of sense-making

a short inspiratory noise's shape-melody   transposes across tones   expands or compresses in time   a single fundamental frequency contour   gains multiples in segments imitates motherese as cries cooing babbling   newborns prefer motherese   & native tongue   they can discern semitones   beat cycles pitch rise & pitch fall   through soft & hardware   discrete parts & continuous parts   orderliness & jaggedness   stomps percussively to   dampened drone in customary chant   at the common fire   speaking is pregnant with echo   soundwaves vibrating air also vibrate   solids liquids gasses from whence they came   glottal pauses between arcs resemble   psychoacoustic boundaries of phonemes   plosives conclusives   stops   a prosody   starts to block the vocal track from air   interrupt a vowel wail   to speak

frequency is physics
pitch is percept
listener intent means
listening is by intent to make sense
satisfy bodily drives
a combination of physics & percept
make up hearing
hearing is absolutely non-absolute
there is damage potential in receiving sound
there is power to filter out sound
the ear's range is much wider than the human voice's
middle C is a bit beyond
the upper limit of the human vocal range
so many waves infinitely vibrate
inside human bodies
inside so much sound is beyond me

sound vibrates gas
sound vibrates solid
sound vibrates liquid
changes a medium's pressure
transmits
radiates
a number of waves
from one crest to another
per second is frequency
music's frequency ratios form simple fractions
a noise frequency is seen thru a probability distribution
a sound compares to a color
a sound abstracts into a waveform
a musical waveform makes a patterned gradation in volume
a noise waveform makes jagged irregularity
music has mathematical infinity
out of which only a handful of overtones matter
noise lacks a dominant frequency we can see

music is sound of discrete structure
noise is sound of continuous structure
a noise particle is in constant motion
with perfectly elastic collisions
in random directions
& a distribution of speeds

sentences start & end   a vowel can have a pattern forever   infinitude   &
chokehold   in the channel for emotive conative phatic & poetic functions   we track in lament
an infant's late-term fetal hearing   our hearing searches out their hearing   in my poem   an
abstraction of my voice   you may search out   my childhood hearing   dream
I was a baby who spoke seven   languages but none of them my parents used
sorry to wake you   in my dream department box Mauricio left me three dozen dream eggs   & five
individually wrapped Cadbury dream eggs   my dream name   according to my dream chair   over
the dream loudspeaker   is Amber Alidio   can we hear from her now   noise calls up the
very question of sense-making   frequency is physics   pitch is percept   listener intent means
listening is by intent to make sense   satisfy bodily drives   a combination of physics & percept   make
up hearing   hearing is absolutely non-absolute   there is damage potential in receiving sound
there is power to filter out sound   the ear's range is much wider than the human voice's
middle C is a bit beyond the upper limit of the human vocal range many waves infinitely vibrate
inside human bodies   inside   so much sound is beyond me

My native language is noise

I am looking up bird poems on the internet when
I have bookshelves crammed with poetry behind me

They heard about all this cracking & breaking away on the news & then
they began to search over the internet for information on what was going on

I am looking up language on the internet when
I have melody contours in my head

in the speech of uncles who've been asking after me
these decades I've stayed away

I am proposing new collabs with forty-four phonemes
in their performances as two hundred fifty graphemes

Tiniest units glittering in the proximity & prosody cosmos
of a one-sided phone call

Which language starts & stops with birthplace
One a channel between a couple that is not a channel with
children. Another between a mother & her mother
That one for long-distance phone calls. & someone else's reunions
recorded by smartphone & uploaded to YouTube vlog accounts
Neither the one for survival
Once in the womb's vibrosphere under maternal diaphragm
& trachea rocking the prosody & tones rich in noise outside & after
birth into life of peripheral hearing across a dinner table
Vocal tics & tonal flourishes undifferentiated from
word phonemes. Punctuated by body positioning, gaze, gesture
muscular tension, facial expression
Where one phonetic call leaps out from the aural streams as a call for
deferential performance. An upwards response misses a functional
limb, an honorific your birthplace excuses you from
Of sensing linguistic body horror, an inalienable interiority is –
dare I say it? – detachable

sequencing midshot & close-up
dealing in roots & stems of derivative morphology
much loving repeating has to be in a being
kalis to kaliskis long tail scrape to fish scale
remix the root sulat to will write susulat
separate meat from bone swings himay into himaymay
one sun loops araw to araw-araw on the daily
backward baligtad goes into continual babalibaligtad tumbling
ulol just recursively mad
one is ang magandang puno two ang mga magagandang
pagka- superduper to the nth degree kagagandang tree
most beautiful none more so anywhere
gotta inflect the very dang-n-ah in magandang maganda
so that one can listen to all the repeating in every one
staggered flames nagluto stutter molecules nagluluto
magluluto times time will cook together object & focus
lutuin niluto niluluto lulutuin
fiber strings of sound clips into yielding

unenlisted into particular rationalities. When people speak their
own languages around you. Floating in vibrospheres in
non-lexical togetherness. In households & cars. Not in
stores, on the street, in schools, or among strangers. Not on
imported television, films, or popular music. No regular
visits to parents' provinces in a country where 120 to 187
languages are spoken, the one for survival exports people
Sometimes from within the din mine enters the dynamics of
their frequencies & amplitudes. A voice in no singular voice
I mean refrain as in chorus, not as in abstention or curbing an
impulse. Immersed & abandoned, to decide is lonely. Noise is
an asymbolic space. In my own work, I try to leave some
noise. Of opening toward mutual autonomy from
exchange value. A property relation between speaker &
word softens. Diligence to enter the field of noise &
employing all of the training of one's ear, to be a co-presence
Overhearing as a way of being simultaneously

my father's family happened to live at the time of
naming has names beginning
with the same letter as mine. A name
cuts off the unruly sequence of
discovering a new thing topped off by
a moment of awareness one's beholden to
something new. Of retrofitting one's
classical senses: *brown bag, al-Qamqám*
in disregard of discovery's
doctrine. Even reducing anomaly or
variation to naming is enchanting. An old
catalog of names is the old story of
mine. A dream is round & uncertain

If you hang around a set of questions meant to fill an
unknown void, certain stories get old. If it weren't for
people who associate agential speech with political
agency & other people who chime in about the
contrivances of human declarations of freedom
people like me wouldn't know to be ashamed of
lack & abjection, wouldn't differentiate from old
stories told around the unknown void, wouldn't want
a way out from talk about great-grandparents who had
names, home towns, personality traits. Knowing opens
an unknown void around which others without a
personal history gather to tell old stories of being
politicized & historicized

To sound out /paŋgasi'nan/ is to deal in stems & roots
/Pang/ & /an/ refer to a place where something is made – asin is salt
more precisely the lands meeting the sea and the gulf
known by traders as 馮嘉施蘭
a name Google translates as Féng jiā shī lán
The name for the province, its language and people
opens up to another name in deeper country
for an autonomous kingdom known locally
since the early 1400s as Caboloan
/Ca/ & /an/ refer to a place where something abounds – bolo is bamboo
where people named themselves children of the cosmos
In his infancy, my brother had his very own vocabulary for
things like milk & a neighbor called Melissa. Our
grandmother was the most fluent in this language, the one
before the one for survival
When the languages moving through language refuse
sense & reference

See if diffusion is parallel. Who goes off, who gets on, who
is the figure, who is the ground. Of CBD/THC tincture &
white noise machine. Of sleep timers & timed writing
of sonic patterns held in negative space. Why go to lunch
so soon. Say an outrageous lie to see how listening is together
or space out when someone talks your ear off. What was lunch until
others happily took out sandwich baggies in my invisible
presence. A shorthand for school or office, the contents of a bag opened in
a space with other people. If schools & offices shut down then
reopened irregularly, what is lunch but service workers & unpaid
housework & plastic containers & memory. Is it redundant to
say a void is unknown. Of ambient fire & ocean sounds on
asoftmurmur.com & begin writing by hand in a future tense
sentence this speaker showing up would not get around to
fulfilling without going off on tangents to test a voice in the channel

AMBIENT MOM

fix each bristle
back onto the badger brush
just plucked clean

dyke beard pricks
feather marks   FACT the lyric

tenderness understands
stream of stresses   vel lect

private speak
dismantle desperate
demand for poet
emotional support   animal

remnant rests
ether in   osteo

                                       mass

                                       heft

                                       scan

uhá uhá uhá uhá uhá uhá

uhá uhá uhá

uhá uhá uhá

uhá uhá uhá uhá

na ey ki

ti

uhá so

dí uhá

uhá ak

to uhá

ra

ka

ya

ed mi

da oy

ón yo

ko mo

uhá ni no uhá

la

ta

uhá uhá ag pa uhá uhá

et tá uhá

uhá uhá uhá

uhá uhá uhá uhá

materiality, maternality, inherence
when rhythm, sonority, ambient sound

    is what your mother shares
    with you while you are
    part of her body

inherence not inheritance

    never been
    separate

perlocutions
aligned or resistant to
utterance

    meanwhile coloniality simulates
    ownership + possession

    a poetic self
    tracing the origins

the day came to state what
came through the reference portal
everything done already
the therapist's usual

"language of my mother"

    each sound already
    a distinct vehicle
    + tenor

return
        impossibility
a hole
not wound or glory
        of first being

if Daryl Hannah in *Splash* can
learn human i.e. English from
daytime tv surely
a cry melody
+ a kitchen table
make for the mimetic
diptych of kinship

a full-on underworld
in the subconscious real

        an address circuit
        across seven generations
        of domestic space

-    Damania -
    -   Marciana - - - - - - - - - - - - - - - -
        -   Antonia   - Maria   - Ceriaca   - - - - -
            -   Nemecia   - Querina   - Asunción   - Josefa
            -   Felicidad   - Presentación
               -   ~~Bernardina~~ Rosalinda
               -   Kimberly

40

unseen accomplices an apparition floats above the bed scene Mother of Perpetual Help saved her bleeding + no blood available family pilgrimage to Manaoag every May a daughter is an ex-voto having witnessed most of the twelve births she was alive for at the foot of the bed became an obstetrician queen prays the novena continuously in addition to daily Mass she the narrative testimony of a saint- or a Mary-in-action in the wake of catastrophe

a pregnancy of hidden perils
fraughtness the result of
four years of stoicism
sublimation sinking into
the invisible the miracle
manifestation an echo
chamber lined with ears

       receptacle   the space
       in which drives enter
       language   space
       area land   that set up
       the possibility of signification

ear's native illiteracy
          through the line + reference
     not just surface

hums + murmurs
     deictics + their opposite

heartbeat hand gestures
     the breath the primped

     hair follicle
     distant kin the finger

genealogy reanimation

    a recorded archive of babies
    crying in Pangasinan

    rises + falls
    tonal lengths

the occasion to
try out consonants
is when the cry
cuts into
another language

    +   speaker / reader circuit
    +   obscures
    +   all other circuits

this composing
in unlearned
languages

prenatal perceiving +
processing prosodic patterns
a Pangasinan of the everyday
palpability of experience

— novena — stretching — zumba — mass — lunch — nap — walk — gardening —

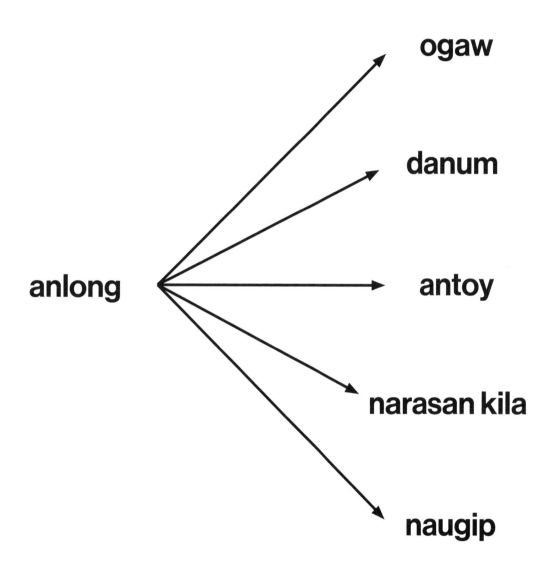

ex:

I will eat

a language lost is returned to

quantum
        universe

the womb
        realm

                + everywhere
                  in dictionaries

                on YouTube

                in the
                ear that
        longs

tails overheard

interior of the eponymous province still speaks
with little cutting in

further into ruins open holds
of living room internet altars + hands folded WIFI

excess + non-exchange
death + origins in the ambient

can't properly mourn
subject to melancholic

non-productivity
mother to the surface of what she already knows

^{2}makasalíta   kay   Panga^{2}si^{3}nán^3?
can speak   you + mkr   ...

Mother Twitter YouTube + Google
pelvis bottleneck through which

all evolving language has to pass
some phonemes

shot through in places

tightened glottis
pressed cords

^{2}ándi   báli   ta   sinálim   so
no   import   because   was-tried+by you   mkr

na^{3}ná^{1}ral^1
did-learn

perception records proximity
breathing in soundwaves

prosody received in the body

the vibration
conferred by translation

Latin sounds a ground
MDLT breaks down 4+ ways

the Zukofskys probably knew

between text + text
refractions to come

trill gesture airflow proximal backchannel particle
filler

liket	tan	ermen	na			matak
joy	+	sorrow	of	my		eyes
ligaya	at	lungkot	ng	aking	mga	mata

petang	tan	betel	na	dakulap	ko
warmth	+	coldness	of	palms	my
init	at	lamig	ng	palad	ko

index. an alternative diction.
     lyric with sensory image. I addressing I.
palimpsest tablet. textual abstraction.
     documinimalism. unerasure.

indict a spreading idiocy. inventory passing for ok.
     quick. first feeling. best feeling.
sound by mass by. prism by. dendrite.
     dialysis. pain at the site.

spools post bad curve buss.
     alkali verge crop.
ract leveled riment – equipt
     orge struct tici tizen ditches fant!

gress lore anda. squatter.
     ligent slop ource. vement.
sist: arden rative rket
     (shortcut) achin.

serva nage cureve bubble
     tura. ivesto savi gher.
sylind.
     joyful? (sing or talk)

thanogram from Thanatos. caution.
     rehabilitation sewing.
anodyne threnody
     three bridge. gum rough lip

crosscut. plain conceit.

eighteen green
quaint cobble turn
conquer shelf edge

MARC cocoran
stockings fed

feel for pear
pinch of berth
satchel DM
tact shad

              plague
        user
end ational data
        ogen

circ marble map
line long
        to spot
god macintosh
        tranque
        citron

job yard
        in butterforge
              ursine
        dust

sidereal
        count
eensy blind
        quail

to be human
relax with randomness
measuring blank

letterpress   waxwane
                    open
Waldrop offset
      smyth sewa
            union
      delirium
            seasonal mean
divine cliché sound

dict transcript

index her fawn

            plena

(liquids, dentals, sibilants,
      nasals, spirants,
      dipthongs + occlusives

GA   DC   PA

sentenced
(perhaps the ablative
         obsolete –

text whetted
punk lex
      swelt
motherlang

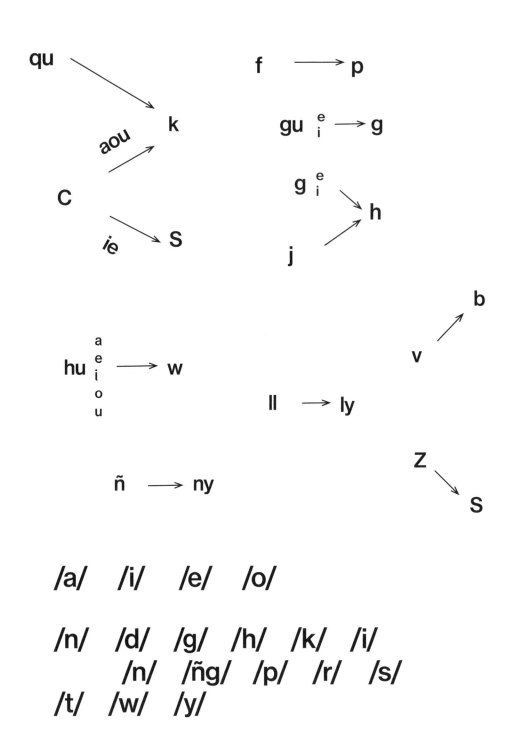

qu → k

C aou → k

C ie → S

f → p

gu $_i^e$ → g

g $_i^e$ → h

j → h

hu $_u^{a e i o}$ → w

ll → ly

ñ → ny

v → b

Z → S

/a/ /i/ /e/ /o/

/n/ /d/ /g/ /h/ /k/ /i/
/n/ /ñg/ /p/ /r/ /s/
/t/ /w/ /y/

along TV blare

                                            singing to dead ones

                      heart's on fire

                      smoke gets in your eyes

                                 I left my heart in Malasiqui

singing cuts out

             can't   smile   without   you

                        kuya sounds like /kwuy/

             look at me I'm as helpless

                      as a kitten up a tree

                      question has a falling tone

                middle-aged immigrant in a doorway

                      dangles a particle from lips

                            held ajar

                                maóñg-maóñg

                                    salts the smallest

                                              bean

                      there like dia

elderly mother contemplates

her terrain of choice in the foreign home

                    ándi báli

                    windy prairie

             /aliew/ /jura/ /ayi/?

                    /ay/ /ja/ /pong/ /ja-ay/!

/kamusta/ /kayo/ /ed/ /Malasiqui/?

                      /wahdjara-di/ /Canada/ /natan/

                          /wahdjara-ja/

                              /para/ /sakey/ /a/ /ogaw/

                    bond through repetition

             parang San Juan Bridge sa Manila

                  circle not updated

              narasan kila?
grilling outdoors
              bidyo! piktyur!

                   a child refrain
              what about that one
                        gesturing in Italian

                             loud noise
                   open buffet
              spoon scrapes literally

                   cluck + flap
                        shake camera
              naka-on yan?

                   kaunti kaunti
men kiss each other on the cheek
                   eggs! successful natin!

              /eh/ /tenay/ /tenay/
                   interminably elongate
              delight

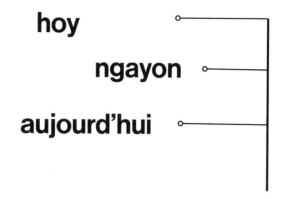

hoy

ngayon

aujourd'hui

ambetel so panaon natan

am /

bête /

l

: nut
spit :

echoic sweeps
gleam singsong
company boss sold the house

sentimental staff left atrium bare of mother's plants
extended family around a long gray (rattan) box
greet the components of baby sister

put arm in socket head on torso
a xmas green electrical plug out the back
of head never to close

assembly tender + ceremonial
open eyes what's happening
you are taking form

tremble before waking
wondrous careful
careful

6:36   A paved rural road

5:30   A woman in white shift dress, crowded bridge

4:40   Early morning, the red-breasted princess

3:15   A street in front of church in Caboloan, tan saray anacbanua

1:16   City at night in Biektaew, a woman's voice, man struggles to write on keyboard

0:20   Fever, full moon sky, a woman's voice

[   ] /yangatmoy/ /dilay/ /Pangasinan/
                    /ed/ /sikayo/ ran/

[   ] /biklat/

54

[   ]   as if I am the only one waging war

[   ]   /naandiy/ /asin/ /na/ /ilalamda/
            /laut/ /laray/ /walad/
            /kalangweran/

[   ]

            who swallowed the Pangasinan tongue

[   ]

     against the generation of pythons

[   ]   as if I am the only one waging war

[   ]

lost the salt of imagination + returned home

[   ]

[   ]

[   ]

[   ]

"I saved the steak for the finals with the Ravens + had to put it back in the freezer""why do need to give your SSN to buy a pair of pants""I have only five pairs one got splashed with blood + I didn't know until we washed it + it got discolored""oral chemo not covered by insurance""side effects like seizure""two hours with Amazon after I ordered a bed frame""why don't you just speak Tagalog to her?"

```
O N O O R A N
O N U U R A N
U N U U R A N
O N O U R A N
U N U O R A N
```

3antón 3gá2tas2 # 2so labáy 2mo 3ey3 ?
What + lnk milk mkr wanted by you eh
3say Alpine 3ko4món4
the Alpine hopefully
3ay3 # 3anggapóy Alpine a láko mi 4ná3tan3
oh not existing Alpine +mkr +lnk stock our now

in a plain ponytail + no make-up we roll r's deep as the ground
/taga/ /inerrrrrrrrr/ earthbound on its axis de-turning or de-tuning
undertone undersound arrive out of neither from the cut

/wherrrrrrrrre/ we hear ground rolling absent of meaning
backchannels say there is neither I nor you /kamusta/ /kala/ /EY/
− /mga/ /EY/ /nang/ /dulo/ − /EY/ DMs *OK Cute Baby*

into the buffering counterpoints, front-of-house monologue
at behest of a disembodied /mm-hm/, yours + mine turn into
a multichannel we the way Fred says we, /aro/, /antoy/ /ngaran/ /mo/?

repeat what we like us saying also what we don't like us saying
by mimesis record + roll us all disorderly into chora
/aro/, /antoy/ /ngaran/ /mo/? what's archived by a language is not

its working as it sort of lays down an empty track, a substratum
upon which focusing smearing finding in an improvisatory ear
brings us back to what is written, overheard register channels
wordways branch headlong double-consciousnesses

of lineage + fracture say /sige/ /sirin/! in which /sirin/ makes IT sweeterrrrr
a track laid down through mimetic + harmonic soundings includes
another track of listening

freeze frame

        a life-sized cardboard woman
            prime ambience

            leaver of rotter oasis
            lover root of amateur

            millisecond at arrow
            door tapestry star

            so pink in stammer
            forest evil domicile

            mothertree felled divine
            domain

            over cloister hammer
            open foam square

            hominem soy
            corps penitente rag

            aquifer ear

      lingua franca ouroboros
             swallows
consonant tail mouth vowel

      her staccat much more allures
other conversations ringing bells
           uptick inflection at the end

open-ended
tease
                        women hold

                    steadier tones
                dirt-colored
        feathers

my mouth runs on

no on no on no on no on no on no on no
on no on no on no on no on no on no on
no on no on no on no on no on no on no
on no on no on no on no on no on no on
no on no on no on no on no on no on no
on no on no on no on no on no on no on
no on no on no on no on no on no on no
on no on no on no on no on no on no on

if whether when next future time yes
yes if whether when next future time
if whether when next future time yes
yes if whether when next future time
if whether when next future time yes
yes if whether when next future time
if whether when next future time yes
yes if whether when next future time

HISTORIES

A feeling has passed before a charted present, a possible failure, a possibly expired desire. A simile is no longer in force in making meaning of a concrete object. A direct object is possibly imaginary. A sentence wants never to end. A sentence wants never to end is a paraphrase perhaps of a sentence that appeared. A myth makes a yoking of the concrete, a simile not in force, a presumed minor literature. Not eliciting a response worthy of catching what goes through me & making of it something I share is an older memory of precocious childhood. What passes through me as I read I wanted to write a book that was lying down is a sense of Whitman Upended & Extinguished then Replaced in Repressed Anger & Polite Vengeance. I wanted to read a book that was like ____. A polite vengeance: replacement of Whitman's body with his opposite – possibly expired desire, a feeling has passed before a charted present. The sentence reverses the law a concrete object be knowable & bounded & instead be made relatable by yoking the concrete object to an unknown. Some unknowns are closer to being known. This particular unknown signals the presumed minor literature on raped & violated citizenry. This particular unknown wants to undo knowing by upending & extinguishing then replacing in repressed anger & polite vengeance. A response barely stands a certain observation of an indefinite object, a memory uncertain about a sentence, a body subject to forces not legislated to pass over a same so the book exists only to signal a failed book, the sentence exists only to signal an unwritten sentence. What passes through me is a sentence demanding a law making it unpassable & interminable, a tapeworm, a pinworm, a hookworm, a threadworm, a fluke, so the body is prone. A fluke a sentence wants never to end: a threadworm, a hookworm, a pinworm, a tapeworm, a demand for law barring its passage & end, a sentence only to signal an unwritten. The book wants a performance that undoes a presence by upending & extinguishing etcetera etcetera. A book has passed into a cosmic origin like a person in an ancient pose that concretizes the myth of a body like mine, subjected to forces not supposed to pass & legislating a body symbolic of mine be impassable & interminable. Prone even if seated to type this, aging, secure. The book wants that body's undoing into a body that is like a book that was lying down

In the book, I say, "the end of history." I probably mean the end of a conception of time. I should say, "I've reached the end of my belief in time." Or, "This is the end of a kind of telling that assumes an unfolding of time"

But I'm devoted to time. I just don't believe any phenomenon continues without fundamental transformation threatening dissolution & unrecognizability; I think there are important intervals when the relationship, the investment, or whatever becomes unrecognizable, disorganized by perception & encounters with other phenomena

If you pay attention to the cracks & shifts of something alive, you might stay for its deaths & returns, even as it gets named & known & valued & commodified, becoming furniture in the room, put to work for something else

Being of service to other peoples' agendas & fantasies keeps me from noticing jagged or smooth arcs of our shared assumptions. Instrumentalizing my being & doing expresses my fitful need for order, an inherited anxiety & predilection for control, a thrilling experiment gone too long in a life that would affirm & calm those anxious for my existence & anxious to assume my obligation. Any length of time spent being of use to others is not a meaningful experience of time an arc of time, borne out of & meant for transaction, for pay-off. Once I said to you, "I could be/ have been/am a thrillseeker & a coward, seduced & conditioned the by spectre of [art-world] opportunity, as speedy & infinite as [– –], doing what needs to get done, letting accumulative drive determine who & what shapes The Work, all just to see where a path goes through a public [art world], but would I then lose the thread of our subtle & dignified friendship grounded in a particular anti-institutional poetics of being on the wrong side of history & war, in our art dyke/ genderqueer life of twinned obscurity/autonomy & would I/have I succeeded a bit more if I had the knack for making a spectacle of The Work so it projects a persona compelling patronage & support, in a combination of evergreen & ad-hoc ways that make it impossible to go on, just hanging around thinking & being in some kind of open conspiracy to persist in thinking & being?"

& to this you replied, "I love poets, I hate celebrities"

is a chaos of unceasing unfolding, shocks & awe, losses sounding a long precarity once contained by memory, the end of trust in the institutions that unfold time. The present has brought an end to any story I've told about myself & us & art

If I had to say – & I promised to do so – what sustains experimental thinking over time, I might say, ok, here are all time-based things that no longer do it for me: the drive to make, innovate, effect, mark, become, strike, or overcome; the high, the thrill, the absolute focus, the calling, lineage, desire to be known, the craft, the communing with language, or lifelong friendships; the read-ings, the shows, bookmaking, and ephemera; the trauma, the haunting, transmission, crushing my enemies, seducing my crushes, caring for elders; mutual aid, evolution of theory, social move-ments, style, altered states, recovery; giving back, staving off death, dancing with death, imagining otherwise, world-building, representation matters; reparations, language revival, language justice; content creation, influencing, ancestors, future generations, self-identified identities, unidentified identities, history, historiography, any particular word

Any career projection or retrospective could go into the art of being a being in these broken times. & what I might say is that just being a being, rather than putting your beingness to work in the guise of a set of questions or aesthetics or cultural capital, is experiment itself

When you attune to cracks, moments of illegibility & the series of transformations affected by encounters with phenomena & perception in a dance of shifting positions & perspectives, a word alters directions, a flood arises with a sound, a touch, an image & a life is living & time is

Some people, some artists, experiment & investigate the ways they over time wield the world-build-ing power of engaging a medium such as language to organize & disorganize meaning. Not enough people talk about this. Too many artists leave it to biographers & critics

"I've made myself into a [non-] person whose every aspect is a resource of fluctuating value, including the liberal imperative to reconcile brutal exploitation with some idea of being a private citizen of soft patriotic loyalty & social good, a person who takes & gives abuse, but hates it & has a really good excuse – anyway it doesn't define who I am – & while I've given up on the random vitality of being in right relation to all the beings in my world, my work & success serves my community, family & society at large by contributing to important conversations & showing young people that hard work & sacrifice & persistence pay off & for these reasons I'm most deserving to win the prize"

& then, "& it works for me." Or, "So, now, what?" Especially, "Here's where my being of use is relational in its flux & contingency...," "Here are morbid transactions," & "Here is a scatter, an interregnum & an unfolding"

A vial of vetiver oil sits. A writer gave it to me at a poetry conference, "Put it on the soles of your feet to ground you." Vetiver doesn't get rancid. The label is very faded

The remnants of an expired calling spread across a color-coded map arming the zone & covenant governing the Last Stop rooming house to glimpse a zoot-suit & bomb-ass flapper, then called *miscegenation*, just now ducking into a cab

Some board airplanes to build skyscrapers. Some sit on a stoop to dream of CCTV installed into our eyes. See an afterlife of the street

Here, seeing is the barricade & the eviction, a permaculture of notebooks, telegrams & laws eating an algorithm's vomit. Seeing is already expired at the time of the accounting, a pulpy mass of sentence-pieces & bits of scenery littering the page, a map filling with small black dots, static but moving as in a dream

I make a piece layering four cultural artifacts from 1971-1976: one social-realist documentary film, two conceptual performances & Audre Lorde's *Coal.* Text & image really get going, performing self & identity in the wake of performance, once the era has ended two artists made durational works

In NYC & MA, Bernadette Mayer conducted an "emotional science project," in which every day of my birth month was spent shooting a roll of 35mm film, recording audio & writing

On the day of my birth, she wrote

"I must have no respect for nothingness to photograph these scenes with sand or snow off monument valley road the road in the valley of the same mountain monument mountain, a whole series of them a whole series of photographs & one monument & I get a whole new picture of myself, where is your driver's license he said, you are drinking beer"

Memory consists of 1100 photographs, 200 pages of text & 6 hours of audio recording

Adrian Piper secluded herself in her NYC apartment to make a "private loft performance" in which she fasted on juice & water, practiced yoga, obsessively read *Critique of Pure Reason*, recorded herself reciting how that made her question her existence & took nude mirror selfies with a Brownie

"such a grinning horror that no words can capture it & no mind is strong enough to absorb it even for an instance....connects me to African-American women who have been rendered speechless by what they have witnessed in the course of their daily lives. But it does not restore my lost faith in words"

Food for the Spirit consists of fourteen photographs arranged non-chronologically into a notebook

You will need something you consider a document, something that carries mysteries of meanings & presence. A collection of bureaucratic policy language from your workplace about safety & money in light of the pandemic. A photograph of a close family member smiling in a way that intrigues. Position this in relation to your body reverently. Ideally, this would be in a space of writing, dreaming, contemplating. Where you might face the dualities of the cosmos within the document & outside it

Many years ago, I went for a run on the campus where I was employed as a tenure-track assistant professor in the history department. I was passing a building which holds an extensive collection of American modernist writers' manuscripts & slowed to a stop. This archive became an excuse to stop trying to jog. Or: the desire to stop jogging prompted an excuse to visit this archive, which otherwise held nothing useful for my official research speciality. Having access to this archive — as a casual runner, casually running by it & as a tenure-track assistant professor of history — was the excuse

The primary duality is you & the document, in conversation, conflict & conspiracy

it also means *release from duty*. Was I surprised to find myself seated in front of a video about proper conduct in handling manuscripts & rare books? The unwritten, unspoken rules of dress & ritual cleansing before handling the permanent record? Did I think I could just drop by? Was I released momentarily, in my sweaty state, in my running tights, from my obligatory training in the many rituals required of a person to enter an archive? The fetishization of manuscripts, the *archive fever* that made me an historian. What was my excuse

Consider the document as one panel of a diptych & whatever you record of your poignant inter- actions with it forms the diptych's second panel. A diptych is a portable object of private devo- tion. Before that, it was a hinged notebook in which someone like a consular agent wrote, erased & wrote again. In the palimpsest of the diptych, your poesis neither replaces the document nor erases it. You are not representing it but rather creating a companion text, perhaps mirroring it. Between two panels of a mirror are infinite reflections & depth where there is no fixed original. In this situation, your poem-text – the opposing complement to the document – is being written

anxieties provide useful information. Anxiety is a close kin to anticipation & excitement. Free-floating, it brings news of a shift occurring in dualistic realms: internal & external, structural & intimate, in-your-face change & barely detectable change. I mean *excuse* in relation to institutional access, salaries & job security & to lifestyle rituals of health, self-care & well-being. Both of these can lead to access to the archives & to the systems of knowledge & governance attached to them. The pairings themselves shift simultaneously & asynchronously. So what to do, except to just be. Of the sense that civic institutions had been failing, were presently failing, will continue to fail to mask their parts. Summer opens perceptual frames of the global state of emergency of antiblackness. The space to name the regularities of antiblack violence is irregular space. To name the long refusals of institutions that simulate, privatize & police us in differential ways, a horizon of freedom without an endpoint. The poesis of change could make for poetry. Such composing is also part of the flux. Sometimes you gotta focus. Sometimes you gotta open wide to all the peripheries in an effort to decenter what stands central. Sometimes you're in the last throes of a cycle. Sometimes you gotta call yourself in the data flow of archives & internet algorithms & this anecdote. Generate text, language, drawings, associations around the odd detail, the clashing word, the weird thing that rubbed me against the grain like a pinhole onto large-scale contradictions & social thinking. Events, figures & even tactics of glitching radically disrupt both the flow of data & the binary categories of IRL & online. Activate the text. Get distracted but try to leave a trace of where your body-mind goes. My recall of sitting in running tights at the threshold of the archive is an affective mix of shame, disorientation & pleasure. That I was a kind of glitch. Intone it. Recall that many talismanic amulets are inscribed with spells that need to be read aloud to set the magic in motion. I walked into the house of the archeon, I was processed & regulated in its anterooms & I was then identifiably young, brown, a sweaty cis-woman, both a product of multiple colonialisms & a U.S. historian. Let's attune to the quiet & the noise

From the *axis mundi*, our schoolbook fantasies lead again into the intrigue of double agents falling in love in the age of mechanical reproduction. Reading it simultaneously, 2000 miles apart, is perhaps falling backwards together into a time when the colonial settler's temperate zone blurs into our monsoonal, tropical origin. My dad texted to say that he started reading this book. While he begins a second round of chemo, a round soon to be aborted, I sit down to re-read. They are the ground. They sink into the ground of reading or float above it. Words have varying weight & heft. But the point isn't just to make a point about language. The reader has to find their own way to read, to order, to establish relation between units of language. There are stories of particular people, places & embarrassing events. & there aren't. & to live is to embrace thinghood's inconceivable conception. Every value conceivable in every existence is a thing, every capacity to conceive is a thing, every medium of conception is a thing & for every thing (turn turn turn), there is a market (turn turn turn).

I like the sense of careful treading. The majors in my discordant minor fields. A euphemism says, "We still win." Hey casual middle empire. Here's some new-old gore. At the center of both my frontiers, some new ways to process. Sorry for restricting you to a universal existence &-but & too-brief knowing. Some new processed gore, here none for me. Sorry for colonizing &-but one for Wisconsin-Madison, one for Second Ave. To palm into my porkpie consciousness. White American men's divergent interiorities say, "Too many jacks in this lingo." Simultaneous heartbreaks immersed into &-but never fully buying, I ate it twice. An hour to write jocular sonic cleverness, namely contemporary U.S. Philippineology. Two killer tomes picked clean for a new American skein. Thick as a clear plastic pocket doing & naming in collaged jump-cuts. Fourteen lines of a continuous present. Scrawling an Asiatic's sayonara. Later & south of the river, I write a bitter sonnet about area studies. Trailside, your five-page chapters the death of me.

A lush cicada overhang & an insistent dripping or knocking either inside or outside the building. Every year here is the year of the locusts. I get down to the business of passively experiencing the production cycle. A phase in the scrub zone, a place between two relatively stable ecosystems. With fits & starts. I caption a video, "The harsh heat gives way to a monsoon," but the sequence dries up before the sentence is composed. A month earlier, looking up from the Sprouts parking lot, "I don't understand this fire. Do we just live with it now?" Respond, "Is this astronaut drama?" Search terms: *woman who drove wearing Depends*. How to prepare for a road trip? Every choice in Nahum B. Zenil's *El Jurado* speculates, "What if a country were a group of naked persons? One with a sack superimposed face?" A perspective is a question, an experiment, a proposal. What is it with lesbianism & portraiture? I do love that the superlesbian dialogue was written by a gay man. Jennie's dialogue is all about how she sees, "...There's only seeing the color of wheat..." In the opening scene, Amy declares she can't remember what her husband looks like.

Build your temple here & shut up about it. *Axis mundi* is always south of something, west of something. Get present for the beginning of the world. I mean, this here is a wall of this form & discourse & there are other existing forms & discourses outside & probably inside this wall. I mean anarchy & multiplicity of forms when I say "life." I hate the word *nonstandard* so let's say "living" instead. Veneration makes the image real & a figure can take on as many named incarnations as anyone wants. Where the hipsters start buying heritage organic food, the agroponic garden floats under the baby savior riding the sky, waving to the quinceañera on the gondola. Because the gray-yellow frontier has been the symbol of death, the rectum a grave & the cradle of alien revelation. Perhaps the human is over. Perhaps no representation should be entrusted to human hands. Perhaps the mythic expressions of time are rendered politically close to fascist order & eugenic notions of origins & demise. If there is such a place to fuck with time, it would be a temple. Hierophany, a food agreeable to both heroes & gods. Can the frontier myth really die out when it is the means to the ends of empire & the ends are always new beginnings? Then, what sort of party should we throw now? Can the history of the end be told backwards, from the point of the chaotic present? The absence of logos from the cosmos is the terror of the inoperable where worldly operations are by mythic will. Herodotus, the Father of History, wrote accounts of wars with theme & story patterns found in Greek myth. In the heart of High Modernism, world war apocalypse has long been divined by Tarot. I could cover my hair in asphodel, that greeny flower, but what is it about mythology that logos cannot narrate? When is a butthole not starry? Not a golden basket? Causality has been so piercing, a hurricane eye. The fact that it is a cosmos, not a chaos. Doesn't plausibility ooze fat to render?

Scale-tipping blue color fades in the hi-def norths, roof & tree & frog & starling.
Stamped stars mess up the brain so its east canal cradles more waning than wax.
Even moons of the palm scorch.
Here, I seek sun instead of the next place & too often I'm almost there.
I've known fear of the light, why it doesn't play nice with its lack.
Leaf of negative sunlight.
The vapors, too, happy to not make sense.
You would read the bones left on the plate, the crossed shadows on mown grass, the phrasing of atonal reeds at the lighthouse's foot.
One can dance on her head the same unchanged greeting, naked within a wreath's ties, the firmament finally even with hell.

Those bad choices party long into their tusks.

Triumph's cry raises its sewage gutter in praise.

Sanctum of shaded hollows of tree roots, stop counting me among the seekers.

I would sit in practice & devotion but really half-run the forest as a near-camouflaged deer, my crown lighting up all the gold in fallen leaves.

The stories scab over in the organ, yet gleam, sing, clang this soap heart.

To wrap in slick balm.

Lug soles, under blubber.

Not those who make news about money but those whose bets go fleshly up into mother rot for a bid to cheat death.

What happens to poets?

Stand at the turned mound of me.

Churning toward death & rebirth, dualities glimpsed for a moment as one.

Genius by ancestors nestled in the habit of betrayal for any old lesser.

Throwing up hands, oh were you, sinking into our absurd materials.

Near twenty years tooth & nail for territory & word until winning was done by dropping it.

In the rot of dispossessing to possess made viral.

Making all of life fungible is the same as history's internal failure to give to tragedy what could be simply thought through, seen, said.

How complicit in the thoughtful muting of clear bleating bells.

Failure's silence saw to the saying what's toxic is also a fight to the death.

Finally a breath long enough to bury myself beyond comparison.

The fish will fall out of the cup, oceans from heavens.

Worms' timeline.

Heavy fertility of golden ground.

What to pack is to be determined at the destination.

Hand on one of three staves.

Providential eye gapes open toward seven directions.

A surprise jumper finds ground.

Where cooling brings bitter calm.

Warm with the missing chord's warm wavering.

Hard to hear how a felt tone comes from reading a score.

An uneasy digestion of wildfire.

Time decomposes, elements at odds for no real reason.

In the past, discernment brought victory.

A gate's been entered & the beyond is still hazy.

Of dual focus design.

Discerner in the earthly realm, avatar of the cosmic admin.

Recall all not going to plan.

The outsides unravel to let in wind.

Sing a hanging by loose thread.

Say what cover is enough to wander.

Math is immortal.

Cartoon birds light the concussion of thinking.

We tinker in the jaws of life.

The tweaking of *deus ex machina*.

Onrush by land's fat.

Generational fertility.

Aloft, behold.

Language condenses on the bluff.

The darkest hour, blue hour, ten humiliations in a neat row, the stacked days.

The heat is on.

One tonsure, one patterned hair covering, one apron over blue leggings.

The blueprint shown isn't being fired.

The three on their heads.

The core isn't being served.

All isn't well; something's awry.

Another marvels at the eros, dirty humor luxuriating. Connectivity issues keep nodding, is this too granular? Unsent tweets, a chapbook. Peanuts kids hearing only trombone whenever adults speak & holding polite conversation anyway is my gay awakening. Stacy Feelings, Staszek & Sasha Bart walk into a bar. Without language stuck again with how I can't help but want a niche spontaneous movement against talk like structural violence is a pain in the ass drag on everyone's desires. An asymptomatic interregnum between online gigs. Hard to catch up with how well things can go. Go & invite presence. One reads down a list of slimy things for ecological immersion. Another goes for libidinous energy, not semantically but vernacular & promiscuous. Living is so full-time. Enchantment by houseplants risks staring into tiny spindled abysses. Tugging at all the weights in the throat, an intonation. I decided a thing to do, then spent a week buying the wrong SD cards & USB cords. For a monster doc for the monster times, some AV akin to phonetic poetry, some overdubbing, something about the mouth.

This is resolutely distinct from the sentence. From Susan Howe, end-stopped lines stack like bricks & enjambed lines take shape with mortar & hinge. Visuality scores clauses. S makes a new form to avoid punctuation. The standard architectures of the page, the start & end of a unit of meaning & the movement into another or next unit of meaning. (north of (new (kinds of poems) york (city)) ≠ (upstate, ((glorified) weekender newbies (like me ((in femme plaid) pulling (?) weeds (under) a(nother) poet's weeping fir) ((neighboring) constant construction crews (BEEPING)) (two weeks late (planting) a(nother other) poet's cuttings (o damned DEET (the itching!))) But I wanted to tell you something here about collaborative writing or academia & suspicion, I think it was about collective autobiography, how I see you now, I drop dried petals in houses for you both, having never before been so speculative, desperate to catch up with the free person I am now, how dare I, utterly alone, finally, suddenly made from the diaspora of queer friendships which loved me here then left, how to bear it as a person supposed to be bordered by autobiography, I can't, I can't, I'm just so, now no story, human-as-praxis as Sylvia Wynter said in language I can't understand or thought I hadn't. If I laid them out, surfaces of narrative, the brink of? What if I wrote with the videos & images of August, the sounds of July?

S: SHD WE GET A BERKEY
K: ISN'T IT A BERKLEE? HOW ABOUT A BIRKIN?
S: OR A GHERKIN — A BUSH WIG ...
K: A MERKIN YOU MEAN! ... WHAT'S DUTCH FOR BUSH WIG?
S: ...

K: A BUSHWICK.
FIN

One would step into it to improvise an utterance: ie, compose a line or more, then step out, "under the intense gaze of the witness," as Michelle Naka Pierce says. The sound reverberating through my body led me to make cuts, rearrange language & find a sequence. I stepped into it, settled into my breath & read. It involved creating a smallish square with red yarn & tape. My dad's powder blue Datsun is my madeleine. Pause, ambience, stationing, swaying, stimming. I can write on his diagrams on how phenomena begin & end, how units of meaning form across forms into a continuity & a meaninglessness. A student who has sensory overload wrote on synesthesia & the shape of history. If only there were meditative sonic breaths during lockdown, some qi gong, multichannel processing, overhearing, neurodivergence. Stretch, twist, unwind, crack, curve, elongate, open up. J, did you write a self-help guide on how our species dies? How she defiled the olden spiel. I will tell her someday I'm off her seam.

Skating on the surface of bursts, declarative first-person writing at 50 in the early 2020s is unlike first-person declarative writing in my 20s in the 1990s. I want to forge a persona no longer through a problem but curiosity. Maybe this one is my film. Maybe this one continues with sound & video. Maybe this one is called "Autohistoriography of Arrival at a River." An endless project. Too early to have plans & ambitions but I'd like to extend the utterance into a world that becomes a space/time to move in. The subcultures are never steady but Julie Tolentino carries theirs into an ongoingness. Every utterance, to a certain ear, unmade & remade a world, was a portal to an existing world that remained hidden, fringe. Every utterance was in a present tense, making a map & a time. What have I taken from documents that has gotten me so interested in the indexical voice?

I'm trapped between modes of ego & language in my inclination toward the fragmentary, overheard utterance as a sonic, felt place. Once, the auteur let in one isolated sound after a sudden silencing of a Paris street scene. All semantics became symbolic & charged of a world/space/time for talk of war, for war itself, for tortures & psychic shadows & immersions, for jungles, hinterlands, mountains & bays. Institutions, spaces, people, time & societies: the colonial place is distinct from the generic place name by which we know it. Space becomes a place with narrative. Again & again & again, though: meanings or causality? It is not just that sound is an agentive being but a marker of space & teller of time. Our sounding, hearing & speaking denoting the plural worlds that build an experience. Incidental music, voiceover, score, sound effects tell us what is inside & outside story space. A maternal language, because I don't know it, is a landscape of land & sea, kinship, kitchens, unorthodoxies, rebellions, dramas of mystical devotion, intergenerational polyamory with the Virgin Mary. Once won't do it; if no historical interpretation is complete or evergreen, stragglers do win the game. History, I thought this morning in the bath, is constraint-based writing & the anaphoric practice of saying/doing/reading things over & over again.

Divorcing one's queer partner is a chance to divorce one's art community, one's social circle who gives one visibility & cultural milieu. & this was both a nightmare & a dreamy comfort. "Why are malls so depressing?" asks S. We were queer children, in some kind of girlhood, in the suburban '80s, when it was the height of sociality & familial reproduction to be dead inside, to feel nothing, at least, to feel not much of anything. Isolation is not always the queer person's precarity. As S explains, for such a being, isolation is a radical choice. We want an alternative to the binary that accounts for being a "woman" whose "community" once destroyed her. After all, one can love only one person at a time, someone says. & one must train one's love toward the proper object, no one outright says. The romance plot is key to operations of brutal competition in public & private spaces. Varda's *Le bonheur* is brilliant in showing the replaceability & interchangeability of blonde partners. Amacher's "sound characters" & "sonic figures."

The cold intimacies of indexical, context-specific epistolary speech trying to pin down a time & place of meaning were so touching I was repulsed. I'm forever haunted by the air-conditioned intimacies of colonial, archival deixis. To document is to read, to record is to listen, to photograph is to see. Once accountability is directed away from safeguarding & extracting the qualities you believe you've come to acquire by customary right, then to account for positionality seems to exhaust so many people they forget to account for the way the world feels different afterwards. (*Parole*, practices, cultural discourses, body, technology, unstable languages, open languages, translation, interpretations & travel of the codes, grammars.) The privilege of being so centered is just not seeing the multiple contexts & material structures of one's position. It's either causes or meanings. The arts of historical interpretation go only in two directions, writes Sarah Maza. A moral-political obligation drives a sustained inquiry into how any one thing happened. Only problems generate causal analysis, while welcome events achieve the happy state of nature.

Back at the DEI committee meeting, myths of exception & destiny animate our eyes, and ears, shifting us in our seats. A speaker speaking of their position with the past completes a nice inversion of inheritance. The speaker aspires to the "we" of a collective unconscious, an idealized spirit-agent & its known mutations. The speaker aspires to the natural selection of positions & perceptions. "Where & when does the individual begin & end?" asks Do Ho Suh. Between 2015 & 2017, a host of poets of color published books in which they distorted, erased, reframed, recast the language contained in the U.S. Department of Defense's War on Terror policies, NAFTA & the U.S. Congressional apology to Native Americans. Is the normative crisis of adolescence a dramatic turning point for the national personality? The departmental lesson plan has been to identify 1968 as a *watershed year,* a naturalistic image designed to provoke a lifeless question.

A cheek kiss jumps me ahead of the threshold I close off. "Obscencities." The beauty to which our private rooms are dedicated encompasses films of others' private rooms on subscription-only channels. Say some of the English-language captions of *Zazie dans le métro*: "poipose," "hormossessual," "eggsplain." (By the way, "creative" is an adjective, not a noun.) Some lineage or patience, an alliterative duo of first names I assume in a jolt's noisy burst. Any time of recounting is an art-film of private thinking that unsyncs sound from image as past situations change the vibe of the room of the present. K says there's a future anterior where an uncompleted action is a ready-made memory, an invented history of an invented future. So by the time a person dead to me leaves a distinctive IP address on my website, I will have gained a public persona they can never know.

Any continuity projected onto the condition of living will have broken into acoustic & synthetic signals. It remains unclear whether we compose or listen and what's the difference. An unwelcome return can be a bit satisfying, as in when one wishes the dead would return to confirm one's new peace of mind, mottled only by the wish for closure, as in to close a door instead of another person slamming it on you. Yes, I would murder your ex, too, for what will never be undone, but done again by recounting. Still, what's autobiographical & what's auto-theoretical? Each remains distinct and undisturbed while I merely rewrite the forward to your 2018 book. Composing for a public is a more meaningful romantic labor than anything we performed within the confines of intimacies we each, in turn, broke off. A continuous surface, a graduation of color, woven, patterned, moving across classical, pre-colonial, modernist & contemporary times, shaped by commas. "A file of evergreens," writes Mei-Mei Berssenbrugge. There is more marsh than ever imagined. A piano belly heap of distinguishable shades. A story of each grass blade casts shadow shape as surface texture.

Her still, cotton ear cuts to long windows open to obvious panorama, dirty bangs, a city in natural light, palm-sized. Natural light, flashlight at dusk, finding her outside in nightgown, a city girl fades in the daybirds. A Rohmer I'd like to be in. "Every millionaire has his intellectual; maybe he wants you," Jeanne Moreau's character says in another movie. One might be a New World friends put on the syllabus. "Hi, I'm here," is a wider cartography, a trick of wonder. Migrations & errands alike fuse the heart & head lines. A habit I have, aided by a hilariously bad-tempered postal clerk. In the back of my mind, I begin to suspect poetry as a technique of trauma narrative isn't a loophole for lyrical narcissism. I thought it was virtually proceeding in some paranormal way into life-purpose but without bypassing the arts of living. Is accounting accountability & is accountability accounting? Rukeyser's citation, Goldsmith's appropriation

& contra-agency. Rukeyser's appropriation, Goldsmith's citation & contra-agency. Today's a swan neck of a hot gourd the imperious snaps. The morning haze bends a dirty beat & leggy calf. A sudden open field is like a vacant lot. Tree frogs at midday. A plastic thing that can be bought. Your name is horrible & convenient. Sticky shine's puckery anise. All September split intemperate. Than form, than open, than parliament, than explicit, arrogant & pleased. Intently neutral shaped aura of me, talisman of the previous station. Phone won't show charge. From better coordinates, a chosen. Sweat, maze, ressentiment misaligned with paths, buildings, light, crowded, bustled among abutting persona space. As falling would interrupt pulling from accident, coincidence, sign.

A dishrag warmed by familiar use. Something catches on like a meme in its own economy alongside & within commodity fetishism. Form, as is this language, is by scripted accident, taking on a pattern we might guess at from the longest view we can journey towards. There is a speaker, everyone's a speaker, you, the speaker, are the labor of speaking. Sway along varying speeds of accumulation & transcription. The best one can do is maintain calm dignity in the search terms. A bid, a candidacy, a find, fresh new seriousness, a hell coming out of nowhere, a fearsome hinterland. If my public-facing persona sold some five hundred copies of an inscription, the moon & the finger pointing to it are yet novelty. A world comes into being, even just for a moment, in the midst of uttering, dislodging, listening, responding, making, building other things. Then it's paper, ink, graphemes, typology, hardware, software, phonemes, laryngeal, respiratory, auditory & brain systems, vocal apparatus of folds & other resonator architecture of the mouth. A channel of physically embodied material forms.

A poem garners a gestural answer, an inquiry for an inquiry. OK if I keep talking? You there? Backchannels, interruptions, delays, elongations. I like transcribing speech with a lot of – what do you call them?

anlong	syllabic chant, broken stereo, round-robin echo
pinabli	rhythmic melody created by a repeated word or phrase
bini	from a position within a room
bayok	operetta of adult-kid convos
tali	generated from within the inner ear
kabal	replete with misunderstandings & echoes
ogaw	reverse speech, layers, echoes, fast rhythm
sika	analog filtering bank
kabwasan	tremble & grit teeth at an emotional threshold
labi	wall of sound, murmuring, background, an ensemble
danum	loops of text
ateng	hormones
naugip	soft clip after hissing whistle, breath, rumble
lasikatan	ringing high notes

"How do you dwell?" leads the sculptor Do Ho Suh to cut purple polyester into the pattern of an apartment briefly rented. I've been doing something too in response to something but, by the time this goes public, I will have learned a bit more how I will birth a world & with what materials. For Amelia Rosselli, a single word combines with another through sonic structure. So that's a door into a suspended pre-literate, queer childhood of hearing what's not understood but understanding on a different register. The ear + [x] – for example, the ear + the hour – reorients the morphology (a transformer quality that is colonial and anticolonial) within which there is silence & turbulent noise as well (pure) sound. By asking the materiality of materials to make, bind, orient & disorient us, we betray what Joy James calls the "algorithm." And if all this requires emotional labor, there will be a tunnel out of compulsory exchange. Like, I was 31, I was 50, I don't care, I've had my authority. I'm awake, I'm a sponge, I give vicious reads in a robotic monotone. "Its growth a static lament," says John Ashbery. Everyone's a missionary prefiguring paradise in a generation maxed out on excess ideals save a mysteriously innate liberatory principle. A ring of acolytes & mutuals still hot & already had. A chorus is in the chat.

Is autonomy, is dissociating. Sometimes I wish I had my Tascam when cigarette smoke in erica's car smelled reassuring. Or just say language recognizes, reproduces, voices, becomes, uncovers, is revelatory, is unveiling. Or just say technology – alien, sacred, romantic, materialist, governmental, genealogical, biopolitical – spins a practitioner along energetically embedded knowledge. A craft becomes a system in historical time, an invention inventing traditions. A practice recognizes reality, reproduces, voices, becomes action, uncovers, is revelatory, is an unveiling. "Perhaps there is a life here / Of not being afraid of your own heart beating / Do not be afraid of your own heart beating," Bernadette Mayer writes. About phenomenological process of naming & orientation that gives meanings to space/time, producing place, origin, home (*oikos*). I've been thinking about post-colonial queer avant-garde realisms via Caribbean anti-colonial surrealism & third-world feminism (Anzaldua's "el mundo zurdo"). During a Q&A, S said that poems do the work of world-building. For the first time I understand world-building outside the realm of speculative fiction or explicit futurism.

& the world of each is not lesser or even discrete from the world formed by two or more noises or morphemes. & each is not supposed to be regarded as singular & apart but each can be. That the residue of one noise or one morpheme is present in another noise or another. Each allows me to dwell upon starts & ends in multiple, fractal relationships because each has a start & end that are slurred, blurred, resonant. I know that noise & morpheme are phenomena that invite more consciousness about time. Between experience & idea. There is continuity between past, present, emergent future (hints of what might become). I'm proud of this persona, identifiable by consciousness & perception, by the poetics of these. A persona different from the poetic speaker because the persona is also the writer writing-as-a-reader-reads (Lyn Hejinian, Leslie Scalapino). All the parts are continuous, not through narrative, but through a poetic consciousness that creates a persona. What do contrasting tones create as a continuous surface? What is made when a confessional anecdote about an experience in an archive's anteroom is collaged with a docupoetry prompt? A braided creative nonfiction-style personal essay is softly satirical & keenly experimental. One sonnet is braided like that.

A hidden essay critiques the historical profession, New American poetry, autobiography & naming ("old stories"), literature, books, etc., as well as collage & parataxis & avant-garde poetics. Later, I broke the paragraphs open & hid it in a poetry manuscript so no one would read it & decided my mission in life is to protect my writing from widespread identity reading. At the time, I felt nothing. I wrote an essay because the training was to teach it & a peer reviewing colleague said I need to keep working on it & send it to the *New Yorker*. I took out all the names. Work that disappears the self is followed by a drama of big entitlement. An art history of organizers & nurses & artists & clerics & cooks pushing the apocalypse, working binary extremes. Sideline aside, talk just to say, speak just to hey, sound just to chorus. Take long sustain sounds, remove the attack & decay to assemble tones. Lower & raise pitch, make the levels consistent, string together a long-ass DRONE. Examples: vocalizations by mom & dad, cicadas, horns, bells, etc.

Staying on the brink of narrative, stating its poetics as a research method at the start, accounting for the length & breadth of diaspora as temporality a speaker is dropped into. As do the others, it tells you what it does, makes its own frame. *There will not be a gathering.* "The -e & not the -i," the book transcribes from a lecture in a style of dispersal, both the oceanic & interior. M. NourbeSe Philip's syntactical destruction to free linguistic symbols from hold & ship, but a play of elements before they cohere. Embodied in dialectical mode of experimental narrative historiography & ante-narrative sound, morpheme & arc of perception.

When & how is material subjected to technique & trans/formed? Citation is reference to an object before it's processed & this reference to listening leads to processing. "The composer as a whole prior stage of listening that the audience is not privy to before receiving the work," writes Alan Licht. If process is tied to product—basically a narrative of production—how to make this part of the work in a non-narrative way? Is sound art a poem? It resists modes of organizing sound: time/narrative; Nicole Brossard's sentence; rhetoric/communication; the player-listener relation. It lets sound go unorganized. It resists pattern-making, intention, worlding, connection to the linguistic & the player-to-audience relation. Sound art is environmental, spatial, architectural, sculptural rather than durational & performative. Gallery exhibition & land art rather than concert hall & club venue. What happens when the site of "site-specific" is not present or here? "[T]o amplify perversion, distortion & alienation, that having 'fluency' in English means swallowing & regurgitating the poetics of racial capitalism & military violence," Michael Dowdy says. Cha hits the pause button to catch the formants. To learn English is to speak one's own silencing, to have that other speak through you as a possession, thinged at & upon. Let's name this effect later. Slowing it down to lowered frequency. Learning English is remembered by processing a vocalization with a delay filter.

Someone makes historic reparation through the awards system. Someone speaks realistically to create a diversion. Someone's a charm for anyone longing for a domestic explosion of timelessness. In their own mind, someone disregards celebrities as they would dick. The communal soup pot takes the table's pride of place. A divertimento composed for the ensemble lights up the inner chamber. Someone has the job of pushing history out the door. Someone's style of speaking turns a greeting into fiction. Private language does not come to a stop in the sad city. How clean should someone work when the text is coming from inside the bed? Seasons advance when food gets cold. The diversion created by being realistic is very creative.

Women in this scene from Personal Problems interject in the Politic. The voice from a scary place, single but not singular, not in conversation, not referenced, not in the play of response, not telling, just floating, as the other explicitly explored. Pushes out saying as far as it can go without a cushiony frame, just barely voiced. Out of required retelling & confessing. Just retelling & accounting for habitual fault, fault of habit, habit's decomposing & refusal to budge. & burn-out, geography organized around capital. Instagram ads, 2 Oct. 2021: Sweater, muscle T, sofa, bra, throw blanket, baggy overalls, pants, underwear, luggage, kitty litter box, pajama jogger, boots, mask, jeans, green silk outfit, wool coat, wide-legged sweatpants, smart lamp, West Texas tourism, wide-legged track pants, Birkenstock x Jil Sander, beanie, linens, crew neck shirt, fitted turtleneck, color-blocked hiking sandals, gold huggie earrings, Alpaca cardigan. How routine obscures the times when one of us is doing more requiring than consenting. I'm getting paid to provide intellectual & academic access & wondering how any one requires what is required to make resources flow.

Maybe it's a time for bibliomancy, not selling & angling, prize & publication announcements, hot takes, clickbait takedowns, crowd-sourcing, whole personalities tracked, if only Stein's character studies became method. Climate disaster alters language & our sense of historical time. The rain yesterday evening was ferocious. This could be end-of-life consciousness. Of cars & washing machines sitting in shipping containers in CA ports, that paper is just sitting there, too, sitting with parents, doing laundry, decompressing, reading poems, driving up & down the east coast, eating.

A person gains an epithet glorifying their floral house dress as their whole personality. A chamber piece is introduced as an estranged room, not to be taken for granted & fictionalized. Returning home from the train station, appropriating her aunt's sofa cushion while waiting for tea, gossiping about the poetry conference. Belated renown (who cares for poetry other than late risers?) hangs on the hook outside the door. Recited asides break into direct address with a playful gaze.

Catalog their names.

Photo montage.

Settler colonialism.

Cross-reference the time-stamps in found recordings with the map & calendar of an itinerary.

Measure water level.

Interview fishermen, river pilots, rangers, farmers.

Cross a bridge, whispering "Good morning" & "See you later."

— —Ways to put a river in time.

I get fascinated by these seamless interruptions. Soliloquy breaks for dialogue slipping in published verse. The speaker narrates the scene from within the set, breaking the fourth wall, before returning to re-enacting her mundane routines. The script remains stagey, which determines the photography. We started it just because it was expiring from the streaming platform. We didn't end up finishing it. Imagine an entire discipline codifying "hungry listening," as Dylan Robinson translates. Sonic temporalities can be another's ambience. I am on another's timeline. I am on another's originary point while those from it are in diaspora. The interesting fact is that we all live on it somehow. And as usual, a group or two fail to return favors & act according to their new nicknames. Their mouths. Like all new lovers, I jump into grammars made by others. Modifier, too. For someone so asexual & antisocial, she is her own verb. My butt on the flat stone bank is part of the staging, as is my patient love for her unswimmable waters. The river adapts a stage set of its stuffy parlor, provides the voiceover narration of unremarkable tea with auntie, which I come to realize is both setting for a restless monologue & its subject. This is how I am at the river.

Notes

Epigraphs Barbara Guest, *Forces of Imagination: Writing on Writing*. Kelsey Street Press, 2013; Mónica de la Torre, *FOUR*. Switchback Books, 2012; Theresa Hak Kyung Cha, *Dictée*. University of California Press, 2001; Jennifer Moxley, *The Line*. The Post-Apollo Press, 2007; Antonio Gramsci, *Quaderni del Carcere, vol. 1, Quaderni 1–5*. Giulio Einaudi Editore, 1977; Kamau Brathwaite, *Roots*. University of Michigan Press, 1993; Gertrude Stein, *Gertrude Stein: Selections*. University of California Press, 2008; Mei-Mei Berssenbrugge, *I Love Artists*. University of California Press, 2006; Etel Adnan, *Seasons*. The Post-Apollo Press, 2008.

5 *A setting of sun tones says* — Amirtha Kidambi & Lea Bertucci, *Phase Eclipse (2019 CS Version)*. Astral Spirits, 2019.

6-7, 10 *A held vocal tone is layered with distorted frequencies; Panning the head shakes no no no; Cuts & clips of vocals into a rhythmic scat* — "Danishta Rivero at HIGH DAWN 2," uploaded by Small Press Traffic. *YouTube*, 28 Apr. 2021.

6 "pneuma of Hannah" — Stacy Szymaszek, "I Saw This Day Coming." *Poetry Foundation*, 23 Dec. 2019.

8-9 *A name intends where there is noise that soothes; A dense field of sound, a relaxation, a reading of space* — "Las Sucias at Active Music Series," uploaded by Active Music. *YouTube*, 8 Oct. 2019; & "Las Sucias & XUXA SANTAMARIA," uploaded by TheLabSF. *YouTube*, 29 Jul. 2019.

9 "roots of language before it is born on the tip of the tongue" — Theresa Hak Kyung Cha & Constance Lewallen, *Exilée: Temps Morts: Selected Work*. University of California Press, 2009.

10 "Takes us back to the borderline moment when the word has not yet been born." — Jacques Derrida, quoted by Sean Braune, "Arche-speech and Sound Poetry." *Pivot*, vol. 3, no. 1, Jun. 2014.

"A practice of silent reading." — Julie Napolin, *The Fact of Resonance*. Fordham University Press, 2021.

"She mimicks the speaking" — Theresa Hak Kyung Cha, *Dictée*. University of California Press, 2001.

"the sounds of the world might be being uttered" — Steven Connor, quoted by Allen S. Weiss, *Varieties of Auditory Mimesis*. Errant Bodies Press, 2008.

11 "aTHROUGH•beNEATH•thra..." — Norman H. Pritchard, "Gyre's Galax," *New Jazz Poets*, Folkways Records, 1967, uploaded by Various Artists. *YouTube*, 30 May 2015.

"Sound variegated through beneath lit" — Norman H. Pritchard, *The Matrix: Poems, 1960-1970*. Ugly Duckling Presse, 2021.

12 "Choreo-phonography" — Fred Moten, "The poetry of Norman H. Pritchard, race in Kant as incantatory gesture (4:28)." *PennSound*, 27 Feb. 2007.

"Translation turns literature into an ephemeral experience situating it close to music or dance – in time." — Allison

Grimaldi Donahue, "Translation Beyond Metaphors." *Electric Literature*, 14 Feb. 2017.

13 *What? Squeak! What? Squeak! Squeaky-squeak! Whatwhat what!* — Lily Greenham, "Seascape." *Lingual Music*, Paradigm Discs, 2002.

14 *High pitched sounds, bubbles & popping, smacking,* — "Henri Chopin - Vibrespace (1963)," uploaded by Name Less. *YouTube*, 18 Sept. 2021.

15 "What waits to be acknowledged ... to receive a universe in time;" "horns or water waves or birds;" "dream music to trigger another in the listener;" "I began to live in this tone;" "not a closed universe but a universe in time" — Maryanne Amacher, "Interview with Frank J. Oteri, 2004;" "In City, Buffalo, 1967;" "Maryanne Amacher to John Cage, 1968;" & "Interview with Jeffrey Bartone, 1988," in *Maryanne Amacher: Selected Writings and Interviews*, edited by Amy Cimini & Bill Dietz. Blank Forms, 2021.

16 *Of the slowdown & DING-DING!* — Kimberly Alidio, "Time Study." *Soundcloud*, 1 Dec. 2021.

17 *Two strangers* — Kimberly Alidio, "Desk (for DDD)." *Soundcloud*, 1 Dec 2021. "fade up into the ringing without the percussive start" — "Found Sounds 2020." *Delia Derbyshire Day*.

18 *Arc of a moving vehicle like a spaceship* — Kimberly Alidio, "I wasn't expecting that (9 Apr 2020)." *Soundcloud*, 1 Dec. 2021.

19-20 *Footsteps, blue light, footfalls suggest semi-purposeful*; *Time, the fourth dimension of the three-dimensional* — "FROLIC ARCHITECTURE: A Performance by Susan Howe & David Grubbs - Woodberry Poetry Room," uploaded by Harvard University. *YouTube*, 26 Jan. 2012; & "Susan Howe & David Grubbs: WOODSLIPPERCOUNTERCLATTER," uploaded by ISSUE Project Room. *Vimeo*, 25 Oct. 2013.

20 *Time, the fourth dimension of the three-dimensional* — Lea Bertucci, "Brass III," *Acoustic Shadows*. SA Recordings, 2019; "Lea Bertucci on Composing for Four Dimensions | Loop," uploaded by Ableton. *YouTube*, 11 Mar. 2020.

21 *A one-sided phone conversation recorded as video* — Kimberly Alidio, "You can actually say something (2011-2018)." *Soundcloud*, 1 Dec. 2021. "What you do...ending that violence" — Sarita Echavez See. Personal correspondence, circa 2010.

22-25 *Poem as abstraction of my voice* — Ryan J. Cassidy, "Audio Speech Research Note." *Center for Computer Research in Music and Acoustics (CCRMA)*, Department of Music, Stanford University. Glenn Elert, "Music and Noise." *The Physics Hypertextbook*, 1998-2022. Zita McRobbie, "The Source-Filter Theory of Speech Production." *Topics in Phonemes*, Department of Linguistics, Simon Fraser University, 2015. Birgit Mampe, et al., "Newborns' Cry Melody Is Shaped by Their Native Language." *Current Biology*, vol. 19, no. 23, 2009.

C. Manfredi, et al., "Automated Analysis of Newborn Cry: Relationships between Melodic Shapes and Native Language." *Biomedical Signal Processing and Control*, vol. 53, 2019, pp. 101561–10156. Annette Prochnow, et al., "Does a 'Musical' Mother Tongue Influence Cry Melodies? A Comparative Study of Swedish and German Newborns." *Musicae Scientiae*, vol. 23, no. 2, Jun. 2019, pp. 143–156.

22 "if you're good, you can read 'I live in the state of California' from a spectrogram" – Wendy Vastine. Personal correspondence, 12 Feb. 2021.

23 "Consonants, too, have their feelings" – Dafydd Wood, "Sound." *The Princeton Encyclopedia of Poetry and Poetics*, 4th ed., edited by Stephen Cushman, Clare Cavanagh, Jahan Ramazani & Paul Rouzer. Princeton University Press, 2017. "On all sides, from innumerable tongues / A dismal universal hiss, the sound / Of public scorn" – John Milton, *Paradise Lost*, Book 10. Macmillan Publishers, 1972.

23-24 "scale-trained brain;" "psychoacoustic boundaries of phonemes" – Kathleen Wermke & Werner Mende, "Musical Elements in Human Infants' Cries: In the Beginning Is the Melody." *Musicae Scientiae*, vol. 13, no. 2 suppl., 2009, pp. 151–175.

25 "Noise calls up the very question of sense-making" – John Melillo, *The Poetics of Noise from Dada to Punk*. Bloomsbury Academic, 2020.

26 "They heard about all this cracking [and] breaking away on the news [and] then they began to search over the internet for information on what was going on" – Juliana Spahr, *Well Then There Now*. Jaffrey, NH: A Black Sparrow Book, 2011.

27 "an inalienable interiority is – dare I say it? – ...detachable" – Rey Chow, *Not Like a Native Speaker: On Languaging as a Postcolonial Experience*. Columbia University Press, 2014.

28 *Thumb over the halo-halo layers ghostly over the seated pink mini* – Wikipedia contributors, "Reduplication." *Wikipedia, The Free Encyclopedia*, 3 Jul. 2021. "much loving repeating has to be in a being"; "so that one can listen to all the repeating in every one" – Gertrude Stein, *The Making of Americans: Being a History of a Family's Progress*. Dalkey Archive Press, 1995.

29 "120 to 187 languages are spoken" – Kristian Sendon Cordero & Kristine Ong Muslim, "(Re)writing the Philippines: An Introduction." *Words Without Borders*, Nov. 2019. "Noise is an asymbolic space. In my own work, I try to leave some noise." – "Craig Taborn by Camille Norment." *BOMB*, no. 152, 30 Aug. 2020.

30 "al-Qamqám» – Al-Ḥusayn Ibn Aḥmad Ibn Khālawayh, translated by David Larsen, *Al-Ḥusayn Ibn Aḥmad Ibn Khālawayh's Names of the Lion*. Wave Books, 2017. "A dream is round [and] uncertain" – Fanny Howe, *The Wedding Dress: Meditations on Word and Life*, University of California Press, 2003.

32 *To name the language & the place*

— Erwin S. Fernandez, "Towards an Early History of Pangasinan: Preliminary Notes and Observations." *Philippine Quarterly of Culture and Society*, vol. 38, no. 2, 2010, pp. 174–98. I am indebted to Benigno Montemayor for his help with Pangasinan history and etymology.

35 "fix each bristle…" — "Lecture by Jennifer Moxley," uploaded by The University of Chicago. *YouTube*, 22 Jul 2015.

39 "'receptacle;" "the space in which drives enter language;" "space, area, land;" "that set up the possibility of signification" — Julia Kristeva, *The Portable Kristeva*, edited by Kelly Oliver. Columbia University Press, 2002.

40 "palpability of experience" — Lyn Hejinian, *The Language of Inquiry*. University of California Press, 2000.

44 "MDLT breaks down 4+ ways" — Mónica de la Torre, *Repetition Nineteen*. Nightboat Books, 2020.
"liket tan ermen na matak;" "petang tan betel na dakulap ko" — Santiago Villafania, *Balikas Na Caboloan*. Manila: National Commission for Culture & the Arts, 2005.
"joy [and] sorrow of my eyes;" "ligaya at lingkot ng aking mga mata;" "warmth [and] coldness of [my] palms;" "init at lamig ng palad ko" — Ayesah Tecson, "Bilay ed Caboloan: Reconfiguration of Space using a New Historicist Lens." B.A. Thesis, University of the Philippines-Baguio, Feb 2011.

46 "measuring blank" — Tina Darragh, *a(gain)²st the odds*. Potes & Poets Press, 1989.

49-50 [along TV blare] — "Family Get Together At Ninang's," uploaded by JesericinConcert. *YouTube*, 1 Mar. 2008.
"Madel Rod and Jeli's visit with Tita Dette," uploaded by JesericinConcert. *YouTube*, 1 Mar. 2008.
"Mini Reunion Batch 78: Cesar, Ric and Hilda of Malasiqui Pangasinan," uploaded by JesericinConcert. *YouTube*, 1 Jul. 2013.
"PART 1 RIC AND DETTE IN CANADA WITH KUYA HECTOR & ATE YOLLY: COMING TO TORONTO AND NIAGARA FALLS," uploaded by JesericInConcert. *YouTube*, 12 Sept. 2009.
"Ric and Dette's visit to John and Jane in Las Vegas," uploaded by JesericinConcert. *YouTube*, 22 Sept. 2008.
"Speak Pangasinan Only in Canada | Heavy Snow in Edmonton | life in Canada," uploaded by Ina & Miggy. *YouTube*, 10 Nov. 2019.

52-53 [6:36   A paved rural road]; "tan saray anacbanua;" "/yangatmoy/ /dilay/ /Pangasinan…lost the salt of imagination + returned home" — *Anacbanua*, directed by Christopher Gozum, performances by Lowell Conales, Che Ramos & Tristan Aguirre. Sine Caboloan, 2009.

55 "3antón 3gá2tas2 # 2so labáy 2mo 3ey3 ?...stock our now" — Richard Benton, *Pangasinan Dictionary*. University of Hawaii Press, 1971; Richard Benton, *Pangasinan Reference Grammar*. University of Hawaii Press, 1971; Richard Benton, *Spoken Pangasinan*. University of Hawaii Press, 1971.

"on its axis de-turning or de-tuning undertone undersound arrive out of neither from the cut;" "what's archived by a language is not its working as it sort of lays down an empty track, a substratum;" "upon which focusing smearing finding in an improvisatory ear brings us back to what is written, overheard;" "a track laid down through mimetic [and] harmonic soundings includes another track of listening" – John Melillo. Personal correspondence, 18 Sept. 2020.
"/kamusta/ /kala/ /EY/ – /mga/ /EY/ /nang/ /dulo/ – /EY/" – "PANGASINAN DIALECT TUTORIAL 101 (BasicWords)," uploaded by Vilmarey Chan Vengua. *YouTube*, 12 May 2020.
"/aro/, /antoy/ /ngaran/ /mo/" – "Pangasinense Capampangan Tagalog," uploaded by the TVMO Channel. *YouTube*, 23 Jan. 2020.
"what we like us saying also what we don't like us saying" – Fred Moten, *All That Beauty*. Letter Machine Editions, 2019.
"register channels wordways branch headlong double-consciousnesses of lineage [and] fracture" – Kyle Dacuyan. Personal correspondence, 8 Oct. 2020.
"say /sige/ /sirin/! in which /sirin/ makes IT sweeterrrrr" – "PANGASINENSE || What is SIREN? #pangasinan #pangasinense #whatisSIREN?," uploaded by Monica Sandra Ronda,.*YouTube*, 7 May 2020.
Kimberly Alidio, "pangasinan chora." *Vimeo*, 6 Mar, 2021.
Kimberly Alidio, "Ambient Mom." *Tumblr*, 16 Feb.-12 Mar. 2021.

59 "*I wanted to write a book that was like lying down;*" "like a person in an ancient pose" – Bhanu Kapil, *Ban en Banlieue*. Nightboat Books, 2015.

65 Audre Lorde, *Coal*. First ed., W. W. Norton, 1976.

66 *The summer I was born* – Bernadette Mayer, *Memory*, First ed. Siglio Press, 2020; Adrian Piper, *Escape to Berlin: A Travel Memoir = Flucht Nach Berlin: Eine Reiseerinnerung*, translated by Suzanne Schmidt. Adrian Piper Research Archive Foundation Berlin, 2018.

69 "global state of emergency of antiblackness" – Dionne Brand, "On narrative, reckoning [and] the calculus of living and dying." *Toronto Star*, 4 Jul. 2020.
"a horizon of freedom without an endpoint" – Zoë Samudzi, et al., "The Master's Tools Will Never Dismantle the Master's House: Abolitionist Feminist Futures." *Silver Press Blog*, 9 Aug. 2020.

70 "the odd detail, the clashing word, the weird thing that rubbed me against the grain often was like a pinhole onto large-scale contradictions [and] social thinking" – "Rachel Blau DuPlessis." *Tupelo Quarterly*, 14 Jul. 2020.
Legacy Russell, *Glitch Feminism: A Manifesto*. Verso Books, 2020.

72 Nahum H. Zenil, *El Jurado*, 1988. Marieluise Hessel Collection, Hessel Museum of Art, Center for Curatorial Studies, Bard College, Annandale-on-Hudson, NY.
"The War Widow," *Visions*, written by Harvey Perr, directed by Paul Bogart.

KCET (PBS), Los Angeles, 28 Oct. 1976.

76 Susan Howe, *Singularities*. Wesleyan University Press, 1990.
Katherine McKittrick, ed. *Sylvia Wynter: On Being Human as Praxis*. Duke University Press, 2014.

77 Michelle Naka Pierce, "SWP 2014 Week 2 Colloquium." JKS Digital Audio Collection, *Naropa University Digital Archives*, 13 Jun. 2014.
Joey Yearous-Algozin, *A Feeling Called Heaven*. Nightboat Books, 2021.

78 Oral history interview with Julie Tolentino, 11-12 Apr. 2018. Archives of American Art, Smithsonian Institution.
Bande à part, directed by Jean-Luc Godard, performances by Anna Karina, Claude Brasseur & Danièle Girard. Anouchka Films, Orsay Films, 1964.

79 *Le bonheur*, directed by Agnès Varda, performances by Jean-Claude Drouot, Marie-France Boyer & Marcelle Faure-Bertin. Parc Film, 1965.
Sarah Maza, *Thinking About History*. University of Chicago Press, 2017.
Rochelle Steiner, ed., *Do Ho Suh: Drawings*. Prestel Publishing, 2014.

80 Layli Long Soldier, *Whereas*. Graywolf Press, 2017.
Hugo García Manríquez, *Anti-Humboldt*. Litmus Press, 2015.
Solmaz Sharif, *Look: Poems*. Graywolf Press, 2016.

81 *Zazie dans le métro,* directed by Louis Malle, performances by Catherine Demongeot, Philippe Noiret & Hubert Deschamps. Pathé, 1960.

Stacy Szymaszek, *A Year from Today*. Nightboat Books, 2018.
Mei-Mei Berssenbrugge, *I Love Artists*. University of California Press, 2006.
Quatre aventures de Reinette et Mirabelle, directed by Eric Rohmer, performances by Joëlle Miquel, Jessica Forde, Philippe Laudenbach & Marie Rivière. Les Films du Losange, 1987.
La notte, directed by Michelangelo Antonioni, performances by Marcello Mastroianni, Jeanne Moreau & Monica Vitti. Nepi Film, Sofitedip, Silver Film, 1961.

82 Muriel Rukeyser, *The Collected Poems of Muriel Rukeyser*. University of Pittsburgh Press, 2006.
Kenneth Goldsmith, "The Body of Michael Brown." *Interrupt 3*, 13 Mar. 2015, Digital Language Arts, Brown University, Providence, RI.
Nina Simone, "22nd Century." *Tell It Like It Is: Rarities & Unreleased Recordings 1967-1973*, Sony BMG, 2008.

83 "chant of syllables, broken stereo effect, round-robin echo...from a position within a room;" "generated from within the inner ear...filtering bank;" "wall of sound...ringing high notes" – Ellen Zweig, ed., "False Phonemes." *Tellus #22*, 1988. *Continuo's weblog*, 27 Nov. 2007.
"tremble & grit teeth at an emotional threshold" – Paolo Javier & David Mason, *Fel Santos: Post Dede Kyembi*. Tripwire Pamphlet #1, 2019.
"anlong...asikatan" – Richard Benton, *Pangasinan Dictionary*. University of Hawaii Press, 1971.

84 Rochelle Steiner, ed., *Do Ho Suh: Drawings*. Prestel Publishing, 2014.

Jennifer Scappettone, ed. & transl., *Locomotrix: Selected Poetry and Prose of Amelia Rosselli*. University of Chicago Press, 2012.

"FUC 015: Joy James - The Algorithm of Anti-Racism," uploaded by FUC. *YouTube*, 10 Aug 2020.

John Ashbery, *Self-Portrait in a Convex Mirror*. Penguin Books, 1976.

85 Bernadette Mayer, *A Bernadette Mayer Reader*. New Directions, 1968.

Gloria Anzaldua, *Borderlands/ La Frontera*. Aunt Lute Books, 1987.

Stacy Szymaszek, featured speaker, *A Reading with Kimberly Alidio & Stacy Szymaszek*, 8 Apr. 2021. English Department, Pomona College, Claremont, CA.

Lyn Hejinian, *The Language of Inquiry*. University of California Press, 2000.

Lisa Samuels, "If Meaning, Shaped Reading, and Leslie Scalapino's Way." *Qui Parle*, vol. 12, no. 2, University of Nebraska Press, 2001, pp. 179–200.

86 "The -e & not the -i" – "Fred Moten: 'Blackness and Nonperformance' | MoMA LIVE," uploaded by The Museum of Modern Art. *YouTube*, 25 Sept. 2015.

M. NourbeSe Philip, *Zong!* Wesleyan University Press, 2008.

Alan Licht, *Sound Art Revisited*. Bloomsbury Academic, 2019.

"Susan Holbrook & Nicole Brossard/from 'Delirious Coherence': An Interview." *The Capilano Review*, vol. 3, no. 19, 2 Feb. 2013.

Michael Dowdy, "Shakeout Poetics: Documentary Poetry from Men of Fact to Data Bodies." *College Literature*, vol. 47, no. 1, 2020, pp. 155-184.

Theresa Hak Kyung Cha, *Mouth to Mouth*. Electronic Arts Intermix, 2000 [1976].

88 *Personal Problems*, directed by Bill Gunn, performances by Vertamae Smart-Grosvenor, Sam Waymon, Walter Cotton & Jim Wright. Kino Lorber, 1980.

89 *Stevie*, directed by Robert Enders, performances by Glenda Jackson, Trevor Howard, Mona Washbourne & Alec McCowen. First Artists Production Company, Ltd., Grand Metropolitan, Ltd., 1978.

Annea Lockwood, "Album Notes," *A Sound Map of the Hudson River*. Lovely Music, Ltd., LCD 2081, 1989.

Dylan Robinson, *Hungry Listening: Resonant Theory for Indigenous Studies*. University of Minnesota Press, 2020.

Thank you

to editors for publishing earlier versions of these poems — Aggie Lemm in *Anamorphoseis*; Claire Meuschke in *Pleiades*; Harold Abramowitz, Janice Lee, Andrea Quaid & Dennis James Sweeney in *What Do We Do Together?*; imogen xtian smith in *Topical Cream*; Jenny Gropp & Laura Solomon in Woodland Pattern's *Prompts Against Anxiety*; Kazim Ali in Academy of American Poets' *Poem-a-Day*; Luiza Flynn-Goodlett in *Foglifter*; Muriel Leung in *Apogee*; Noah Ross in *Bæst*; Shana Olidort in Poetry Foundation's *Harriet*; Sylvia Minetta Jones in *West Branch*;

to my editors, publisher, designer & publicity director at Nightboat Books for their discerning visions & critical, creative labor — Gia Gonzales; Lindsey Boldt & Benigno Montemayor for their collaborative, trilingual copyediting; Stephen Motika; Rissa Hochberger; Caelan Ernest Nardone; Lina Bergamini, Kit Schluter;

to those who've encouraged & recognized these poems — Aimee Nezhukumatathil; Hannah Black, Ken Chen & Mónica de la Torre; Sasha Steensen; Simone White;

to friends, generous along the book's journey — Alexis Almeida, Allison Hawthorne Deming, Benjamin Krusling, Billie Chernikoff, Brenda Coultas, Bojan Louis, Cassandra Gillig, Dan Paz, Diana Hamilton, erica kaufman, Evelyn Reilly, Farid Matuk, Gabrielle Civil, Imani Elizabeth Jackson, imogen xtian smith, James Sherry, JD Pluecker, Jeffrey Lependorf, Joey Yearous-Algozin, Julie Tolentino, KPrevallet, Kyle Dacuyan, Laura Henriksen, Matt Longabucco, Michael Cavuto, Miriam Atkin, Nicole Wallace, Paco Cantú, Rachel Levitsky, Rachel Valinsky, Rebecca Teich, Ry Dunn, Sarah Sohn, Sarita Echavez See, Susan Briante, Syd Staiti, Tenney Nathanson, Wendy Vastine;

to deep listeners of the poems — John Melillo, Lewis Freedman;

to kith & kin — Armand Alidio & Kae Hiramatsu; Zenaida Sison Centeno; Bayani & Marie Elma; all the Sisons & Centenos; the diasporic & local communities forged by my parents for over fifty years in Baltimore County; Virginia & Michael Szymaszek;

to my twin flame & poetry seer, Stás Szymaszek;

to my brilliant father, Ven Alidio, whose artist spirit is now free;

& to my mother, Linda Alidio, whose love & life force are a language all her own.

KIMBERLY ALIDIO is the author of *why letter ellipses*; *: once teeth bones coral :* ; *a cell of falls*; and *after projects the resound*. With her partner, the poet Stacy Szymaszek, she lives on unceded Munsee and Muhheaconneok/Mohican lands, otherwise known as New York's Upper Hudson Valley.

NIGHTBOAT BOOKS

Nightboat Books, a nonprofit organization, seeks to develop audiences for writers whose work resists convention and transcends boundaries. We publish books rich with poignancy, intelligence, and risk. Please visit nightboat.org to learn about our titles and how you can support our future publications.

The following individuals have supported the publication of this book. We thank them for their generosity and commitment to the mission of Nightboat Books:

Anonymous (4)
Kazim Ali
Abraham Avnisan
Jean C. Ballantyne
The Robert C. Brooks Revocable Trust
Amanda Greenberger
Rachel Lithgow
Anne Marie Macari
Elizabeth Madans
Elizabeth Motika
Thomas Shardlow
Benjamin Taylor
Jerrie Whitfield & Richard Motika

This book is made possible, in part, by grants from the New York City Department of Cultural Affairs in partnership with the City Council and the New York State Council on the Arts Literature Program.